Emerging Issues and Challenges in North-East India

Emerging Issues and Challenges in North-East India

Editors
Jesmine Ahmed
Rita Saikia
Niranjan Mohapatra

KALPAZ

First Published, 2020

Published by

Kalpaz Publications
C-30, Satyawati Nagar,
Delhi - 110052
Ph.: 011-47034999, 9811692060
www.kalpazpublications.com
E-mail: kalpaz@hotmail.com

Printed at: G. Print Process, Delhi

Cataloging in Publication Data—DK
Courtesy: D.K. Agencies (P) Ltd. <docinfo@dkagencies.com>

Emerging issues and challenges in North-East India /
[editors], Jesmine Ahmed, Rita Saikia, Dr. Niranjan Mohapatra.
pages cm
Contributed articles.
Includes bibliographical references.
ISBN 9789353242497 (HB)

1. India, Northeastern—Politics and government. 2. India, Northeastern—Social conditions. 3. India, Northeastern—History. I. Ahmed, Jesmine, editor. II. Saikia, Rita, editor. III. Mohapatra, Niranjan, editor.

LCC DS483.E44 2020 | DDC 954.1 23

Contents

Preface

North East India is a land of swelling hills and plains with lavish green cover and a wide variety or rare and exotic flora. It is famous for its rich cultural heritage, socio-economic and ethnic diversity and rich natural resources. The North-East, which is known for its pure beauty, lush green forests and rich biodiversity, is at a risk of getting exhausted perpetually. North-East India constitutes an important ecological region in the country. Also known as the land of the seven sisters, a metaphor for its seven states- Arunachal Pradesh, Assam, Mizoram, Nagaland and Tripura, the region houses over a hundred tribal communities characterized by diverse linguistic, political and religious backgrounds. The region is the home of extraordinarily diverse mosaic of ethnic groups having distinctive social, cultural and economic identity, more akin to their South Asia neighbors than main land India. Being one of the most neglected regions of the Indian union, overall state of affairs in the region is quite alarming. The unattended issues and problems of the past are being accumulated, multi-layered and have become multifarious. The region has become very sensitive and conflict affected area due the growing awareness and assertion of separate ethno-political identity of numerous ethnic peoples. The region has more issues to be addressed and challenges to face than any other parts of the country. This area is very resourceful in respect of natural resources and bio-diversity. In spite of these advantage the North-East region is lacking behind in development in comparison to the most of the states of India because of the tension prevailed in North-East region. North-east

India is characterized with illegal international migration, cross border terrorism, insurgency, ethnic movement and conflict in respect of mutual boundary among the North-eastern states.

The present book is covered with the rising issues and challenges of North-east India which would create hindrances in the development of the region. The book is consisted with the eleven articles which are provided by our contributors. All the articles of the book try to focus on the present up-and-coming issues of North-East India. Issues like NRC, regional politics, ethnic conflict, untouchability, globalization, educational problems, environment movement, look east policy have been discussed in this book. We are very grateful to our contributors who have sent their writings on time to us. The book "Emerging Issues and Challenges in North-East India" is tried to introduce the issues and challenges of North-East India in front of the readers. With this we try to make this book resourceful and hope this effort will create a vibrant atmosphere of understanding and unity and prosperity in the North-East region.

Editors
Jesmine Ahmed
Rita Saikia
Dr. Niranjan Mohapatra

Acknowledgements

The editors would like to thank all the authors for their contributions on time. Without their co-operation this work might not be achievable. Our sincere gratitude goes to the individual author who has contributed the chapters according to his/her expertise for this book. The editors extended their gratitude to Kalpaz Publications, New Delhi who has agreed to publish the book without any delay. Last but not the least the editors has acknowledged the help extended by the library staff of Assam University, Diphu campus for their cooperation for editing the book.

Editors

Jesmine Ahmed
Rita Saikia
Dr. Niranjan Mohapatra

Chapter - 1

The Issues and Challenges of National Register of Citizens (NRC) Updation in Assam

— ***Nilakshi Das***

Introduction

The illegal migration to the North-Eastern States, particularly to Assam from the neighboring countries has been perceived as a serious threat. The people of the State demands solution to the vexed issue not only politically but administratively and socially too. The Assam Accord, which was signed between the Government of India and AASU leaders after the Assam Movement in order to deport foreign nationals also failed to make an impact because of its poor implementation strategies. The Vote-Bank politics of the political parties can mainly be attributed for its failure. The sad fact is that the problem of illegal migration has turned worse with the passage of time. The student leaders of the AASU who later formed AGP Government and ruled Assam for two terms showed their pathetic lack of will to address the issue during their tenure. As a result of the growing problem of illegal influx in the state the National Register of Citizens (NRC) is carried out under the Supreme Court's guidelines. The updated NRC has to include the names of those persons or their descendants who appear in the NRC, 1951, or in any electoral rolls up to the midnight of March 24, 1971.[1] The entire process of NRC updation includes many phases like publication of Legacy data, distribution of receipt of application forms, verification of the persons, publication of the draft NRC, receipt of claims and objections and publication of the final NRC. NRC Seva-Kendras are made everywhere to systematize the whole process and to help the citizens' matters relating to it. In Aug 31, 2015 the form submission of NRC has been completed successfully.

The NRC of India was prepared after the 1951 Census by recording particulars of all the persons enumerated during the census. The Register was kept in the offices of the Deputy Commissioners and the sub divisional officers as per the Government of India instructions. In 1960, the same was transferred to police. For updating the register, the central Government is required to provide guidelines and funds and implement the same through the State Government machinery under the direct supervision of the Registrar General of India. So far, the NRC is not updated in other parts of the country except the ongoing exercise in Assam. The purpose of the exercise is to determine the illegal migrants in the State and then to take further steps regarding it. The basic objective of the updation of NRC is to ensure that the names of foreigners, illegally enrolled in the voter's list as Indian citizens are deleted and an authenticated and foolproof NRC should be prepared. The present exercise is undertaken as per the memorandum signed between Government of India and AASU in the year 1985.[2]

The Governor of Assam, PB Acharya said that a correct NRC and Voters' list free from names of any foreigners' is vital for the security of not only North-East region but also of the entire country.[3] He further expressed that voters' list of 2015 can be a supplement to NRC but it cannot be the basis of it. The officers engaged in the updation process must have careful to ensure that no names of foreigners are included in the NRC. Updated NRC would be a legal document for determining citizenship for all time to come and it would help in the detection and deportation of the immigrants who entered Assam illegally.

The Nodal officer Pratik Hajela, who is in the charge of NRC updation process said that it would take serious steps while receiving the forms so that no one can give fraud document in this regard.[4]

There was a controversial situation arising in the updation of NRC in Assam. Under this controversial situation and long debate under the orders of the Supreme Court of India, the Government of India has started the process of updating the NRC of 1951. The objective of updation of the NRC is to identify foreign nationals living in the state illegally and to deport them from the state to ensure security for the native people. There was an apprehension among civil liberty groups that the process of updating NRC might not be fair and result in non-inclusion of the Muslim minorities and Hindu Bengalis who are often suspected to be illegal citizens. Political Parties and other organisations present in the State are also playing the drums in different beats on the updation issue of NRC.[5]

Issues and Challenges of NRC Updation in the State

The NRC supposed to be updated from time to time. But the Government of India did not pay any attention to update the NRC of Assam. The NRC updation is a long standing demand made by the civil and socio-political organizations like All Assam Students Union (AASU), Krishak Mukti Sangram Samiti (KMSS), Akhil Bhratiya Vidyarthi Parishad (ABVP), Assam Jatiyatabadi Yuva Chatra Parishad (JYCP), Assam Public Works (APW), and many other Organizations. They demanded the Government to update the long pending NRC of 1951 and they believed that the updation of NRC 1951 would segregate the foreign nationals living in the State from the Indian citizens. After a long debate and with the interference of the Supreme Court of India, the Government of India through a notice had decided to update the long pending NRC of 1951. It is said that updated NRC would be an instrument to identify the infiltrators from Bangladesh into the Assam. The NRC is expected to be a reference point against which an individual can check his/her citizenship status.[6]

According to the former Chief Minister of Assam, Mr. Tarun Gogoi, "NRC updating will bring to end issues revolving around the State's biggest problem of infiltration from Bangladesh. There are people who believe that infiltration (from Bangladesh) is still going on despite erection of a barbed wire fence and intensified BSF patrolling along the border."[7]

The Government of India has launched two pilot projects in revenue circle of Barpeta District and Kamrup District.As per this all the residents where most of the people were illiterate were asked to apply before the district magistrate along with several supportive documents, appear for hearing and prove their citizenship to the satisfaction of the officer concerned for inclusion of their names in the updated NRC. The task of Pilot Project of updating the NRC, 1951 started on 15th June 2010 in Barpeta Revenue Circle. The copies of NRC 1951, Electoral Rolls of 1961 and 1971 were to be reprinted by the district authorities. But the district authorities failed to reprint the documents in full.

Moreover, there were numerous anomalies and confusions in the documents which were made available for the public.[8] In some cases only the surnames and titles had been printed instead of full name. In some other cases siblings were mentioned as *Kesua* (babies) and "*Amuk*' (Somebody). Males were shown as wives and females were marked as husbands, many mistakes were found in the reprinted NRC of 1951. Even the birth places of a large number of people had been shown as to be Mymenshing, Dacca and West Pakistan though their original birth place is of different places of Assam.[9]

Due to the problem found in the mechanism of the NRC updation process, the 'All Assam Minority Students Union' (AAMSU) protested before the Deputy

Commissioner's Office, Barpeta, on 21st July 2010. They have demanded the immediate postponement of the pilot project of the ongoing updation of the NRC. The organization also demanded the settlement of the D voters' problem before starting the process of NRC updation. Thousands of processionists coming from different areas of District approached the DC office on 21st July, 2010. The leaders of the processionists wanted the Deputy Commissioner to come out of his office and take their memorandum which the later denied. In that time a third party was ready with stones to attack the DC office. After that the mob now lost their nerves and became violent and in return started pelting the same stones to the DC office. Suddenly, the Superintendent of Police of the district appeared on the scene and ordered the police personals for firing on the mob. It resulted in the loss of lives of four people and injured many people too. The passed on people were Siraj Ali, 25, Majam Ali, 55, Matleb Ali and Moidul Mullah, both 30.The police could have controlled the situation by applying tear gas or *lathicharge*. Even after the firing some of the processionists have tried to run away but later they were caught by some unidentified youths and beaten up badly. One of the victims namely Anowar Hussain age 35 told in front of the Telegraph that he was beaten up by some unidentified youths. In spite of his request he was not released by them until he became unconscious.[10]

The town also witnessed clashes between the protesters and residents, who started attacking the AAMSU supporters allegedly for shouting anti-AASU and anti-'Tarun Gogoi' slogans. The situation became out of control. Finally with the help of security forces the condition came under control and it resulted in the postponed of NRC updation in the State. The State Government then immediately announced the postponement of the NRC updation process in the State.

In spite of this, AASU demanded the updation of NRC would be done immediately as its basic purpose is to detect the illegal migrants. Though the Pilot Project failed, the process of NRC updation could not be stopped. The Barpeta incident delayed but modified the process of NRC updation. Many of the anomalies of the Pilot Project were modified and process of NRC updation works under direct supervision of the Supreme Court has started in 2015. The Government of India has made the following mechanism for the NRC updation works. On the basis of the Assam Accord 1985 the NRC is updated as per the provisions of the Citizenship Act, 1955 and the Citizenship (Registration of Citizens and Issue of National Identity Cards) Rules, 2003.[11]

Following are the list of admissible documents in the process of updation of NRC-

Legacy Data-

1. 1951 NRC,
2. Electoral Rolls up to 24th March (Midnight), 1971,

The above documents are collectively called Legacy Data. There is a list of other admissible documents in case someone's name is not found in the Legacy Data, then the applicant may also produce any of the following documents listed below claiming inclusion in NRC :

List of other documents admissible for inclusion in revised NRC-

3. Land records including tenancy records of relevant period up to midnight of 24th March, 1971,
4. Citizenship Certificate issued by competent authority up to midnight of 24th March, 1971,
5. Permanent Residential Certificate issued from outside the State up to midnight of 24th March, 1971,
6. Refugee registration certificate issued up to midnight of 24th March, 1971,
7. Passport issued by the Government of India up to midnight of 24th March, 1971,

8. Insurance policies (LICI) of relevant period up to midnight of 24th March, 1971,
9. Any license/certificate issued by the Government authority of relevant period up to Midnight of 24th March, 1971
10. Document showing service/employment under Government/Public sector undertaking up to midnight of 24th March, 1971,
11. Bank/Post office Accounts of relevant period up to midnight of 24th March, 1971,
12. Birth certificates issued by the competent authority up to midnight of 24th March, 1971,
13. Educational certificate issued by Board/ Universities up to midnight of 24th March, 1971,
14. Records/ processes pertaining to court up to midnight of 24th March, 1971.[12]

The documents placed below are only supporting documents and would be accepted only if the person do not have any of the above mentioned document then he can produce one of the following document, which has been accompanied by any one of the admissible documents listed above.

(a) Certificate issued by the Secretary of the Village Panchayat countersigned by the local Revenue official in respect of females from rural areas who have migrated to other is only optional and not mandatory.

(b) Certificate issued by Circle Officer in respect of females who have migrated from an urban area after marriage is only optional and not mandatory.

(c) Ration Cards issued by competent authority with official seal and signature up to 24th March, 1971.[13]

Although pilot project was failed but NRC updation has done in a disciplined manner. Some issues are come on the way of it. The issues and challenges which have come in the updation process of NRC are discussed below.

Vote Bank Politics of Political Parties

The Vote bank politics of the political parties play a significant role in the process of updation of NRC. The Supreme Court continues to deal with the Indo-Bangla border management in Assam. Assam has faced problem because of the cross-border infiltration from the Bangladesh over the decades. The Apex Court's directive in July after it had accepted the findings of its Commissioner's report on Indo-Bangla border was a disappointing one. This report shows the inactiveness of the both Centre and State Government's role in this issue. Therefore the court ordered constitution of a coordination committee which would deal with the all issues neglected by the Governments.[14]

The apex court appointed commissioner's report, noted that there was no patrolling of the riverine border stretch in the Dhubri sector and in Silchar sector as well as the floodlights were not in operational action. Again there was no patrolling by State Police at stretches or any kind of fencing there. This helps the infiltrators to move freely in the border areas. The court ordered to set up of another Sixty Four Foreigners Tribunal (currently it is now 36 FT with inadequate infrastructure and manpower) to handle the pending cases which is approximately five lakhs.[15] In this regard it can be seen that the State Government has some hidden interest on the illegal migrants. This is nothing but the Vote-Bank politics of the Both State Government and The Central Government which make them insincere in checking the illegal influx as well as the detection and deportation of the foreign nationals from the country.

The signing of the Assam Accord which is a Memorandum of settlement in the year 1985 was hoped to solve the issue of illegal migration. But the sad part is that till date it is not implemented in the proper sense by the Government. As a result more and more illegal migrants are crossed the porous border to enlarge the vote-bank of the ruling party. The *United Progressive Alliance* (UPA) Government during its stay in Power for a long period at the Centre did not give any kind of interest in the implementation of the Assam Accord. The motive behind it was that the Congress Government of Assam could be in power for a long time depending on the vote bank of the Foreign Nationals. Therefore, they are not concerned about the large scale infiltration caused by the foreign nationals from Bangladesh.[16]

Like UPA, BJP in its election manifesto of 2014, claimed that if they come in to power then they would look into the matter of illegal migration from Bangladesh in Assam and take all the measures to solve this problem. But after getting power, the *National Democratic Alliance* (NDA) Government has not taken any serious step in solving this issue. People hoped that at least after Indo-Bangla land exchange deal, the NDA Government would seal the borders and implemented the other causes of Assam Accord. But it is found that the committee appointed by Supreme Court as *Upamanyu Hazarika Commission* submitted its report as large portion of the border remains as open, unchecked and no action has been taken by the Governments.[17] Instead of it the Central Government has decided to settle lakhs of Hindu Bangladeshi migrants, who have been infiltrating into Assam until March, 2014.[18]

The *Illegal Migrants (Determination Tribunals)* was established in the year 1983. At first the State Government has set up 20 IM (D) Ts. The IMDT Act was amended in the year 1988. Before it the IM (D) T along with the Foreigner Tribunal took up the cases of suspected foreigner in the year 1985. Although it took up the cases but the performance of it is like the following-

Table 4.1: The performance of the IM (DT) during various time periods is summarized below.

Period	*Cases Referred*	*Cases Disposed*	*Cases pending (cumulative)*	*Number of Persons declared as foreigners*	*Number of declared foreigners pushed back/deported*
1985-90	22682	6486	16196	6724	521
1991-95	3488	7335	12349	2577	792
1996-2000	17623	4420	25552	902	179
2001-July 2005	68998	5780	88770	2643	55
Total	112791	24021	88770	12846	1547

**Source:* Kashya Nilim Akash(2014), *AASU-Swapna, Duswapna, Itihaax*, Guwahati: Assam Publishing Company, P. 264.

Later these cases are transferred to the foreigner's tribunals. Again in the foreigner's tribunal these cases are not taken seriously. It can be seen from the following table-

Table 4.2: Foreigners Tribunal Cases.

Period	*Cases referred*	*Cases disposed*	*Cases pending (cumulative)*	*Persons declared as Foreigners*	*No. of declared foreigners pushed Back/deported.*
1985-90	32991	15929	17062	14801	133
1991-95	482	5909	11635	4005	267
1996-2000	2986	3552	11069	6026	235
2001-2005	6094	2216	14947	4593	39
2006- July 2012	65666	45456	35157	12913	221
Total	108219	73062	35157	42338	895

**Source:* Nilim Akash Kashyap(2014), *AASU-Swapna, Duswapna, Itihaax*, Guwahati: Assam Publishing Company, p. 265.

The consolidated total of deported or pushed back illegal migrants on being declared as foreigners by IM (D) Ts and Foreigners Tribunals collectively till July 2012 was 1547+895=2442, From this it can be found that the Government tries to protect the illegal migrants because of their vested interest of Vote-Bank.[19] In the present time the acceptance of the Hindu migrants from Bangladesh is nothing but the Hindu Vote-Bank politics of the NDA Government.[20]

D Voter's Issue

'D' means that the citizenship status of the elector was *doubtful / disputed.* Verification was done through local verification officers (LVOs). Based upon the report of the Local Verification Officers (LVOs), the Electoral Registration Officers took a decision on whether a reference to the concerned Tribunal was necessary to ascertain the Indian citizenship status of such elector. Once the Electoral Registration Officers confirmed in the affirmative, such cases were forwarded to the competent authority (SP of the concerned district) for reference to the concerned Tribunal. Such electors marked with 'D' were neither permitted to cast their votes nor contest in Elections.[21] It is done when the Election Commission of India has done revision of electoral roll in Assam in 1997 on January 5, 1998, the letter 'D' was marked against the names of those electors who could not prove their Indian citizenship status at the time of verification through officers appointed for that purpose.

In 1997 the election commission of India identified a section of Muslims live in the Char Chapari areas of Assam, linguistic Hindu minority and even the Rajbongshi people of the state as 'D'voters.[22] The process of identification of 'D' voters was unusual. It is alleged that the lower officials of Election Commission were asked to mark at least 10 to 20 people in each village of the state as 'D' citizens. Thus in many families wives or husbands became doubtful citizens keeping rest of the members Indians. Again in some families, sons and daughters were identified as doubtful citizens, where, their parents remained Indians.[23]

The officials did not follow any criteria for selecting the "D" Voters. The people who have denied of their franchise rights are considered as "D" Voters. There are 3.7 lakhs people are considered as D Voters by the officials of the Election Officials. In the Foreigners' Tribunals many D voters' cases are registered. But only few cases are settled in the foreigners' tribunal such as during 2006-

2010 in the foreigners' tribunal of Bongaigaon, against 9,222 registered cases only 1,333 got settled and four accused have been identified as illegal migrants from Bangladesh. Likewise in the Foreigners' Tribunal of Goalpara District, against 22,000 'D' voters cases only 6,00 have been settled till date and only one women called Tarabhanu has been identified as foreigner.[24] This case made a huge controversy as people believed that she was of Indian origin but failed to prove it. She was taken away from her three years child and deported from the State. It seems the inhuman nature of the State.

The foreigners' tribunals must work in a proper sense to solve these 3.7 lakhs cases of D voters. Otherwise the children of the D voters are waiting for years and years to get their citizenship back. Apart from this, the interesting fact is that the solved cases of D voters, who were given the status of Indian citizens, they have not included in the voters list yet.

Following table summarizes the disposal of D voters' case by the Tribunals since 1998.

Table 4.3: 'D' VOTERS (1998-July, 2012)

Cases referred	*Cases disposed*	*Cases pending*	*Persons declared as foreigners*	*Persons declared as Indian*	*Cases where no opinion could be expressed*
231657	88192	143465	6590	44220	37382

*Source: Nilim Akash Kashyap (2014), *AASU-Swapna, Duswapna, Itihash*, Guwahati: Assam Publishing Company; P. 270.

The term D voters have not been explained or defined in any of the statute in India nor the General Clauses of the IMDT act. The term D-voter is a creation of State machinery and due to the defaults of enumerator during enumeration. The concept and definition is not even known to the many fellow citizens of this country. This is the routine problem of Indian citizens in Assam. In fact The Assam Accord which explained the foreigner issue from clause 5.1 of the Accord to clause 5.9 but silent about the D-Voters, its talks about the detection and deportation of illegal migrants. There is no laid down procedure to declare citizens as "Doubtful Voters" by the appropriate authorities and to debar them from voting right in the world's largest democracy i.e. India. This is done only in Assam itself. Such provision is not in force in any other State of India, which violates the fundamental right guaranteed by the Constitution of India. The "Doubtful Marks" against the names of genuine Indian citizens in the voter list by the State machinery are being done in the offices, without any field survey and physical inspection. Therefore, as a result some of the genuine India citizens have harassed due to the administrative fault by making themselves as the "Doubtful Citizens".[25]

In the updation of NRC the basic concern is that whether the D voters can apply or not in the NRC. The Government permitted the D voters to apply in the NRC. For example in an interesting move, the Cacher District Administration has said that along with the Normal applicants to the NRC, the D voters can also apply in the NRC.[26] These D voters are harassed by the State Government. In a news published in Assam Tribune dated Aug 11, 2015, Tuesday; The BJP blamed the ruling party to harass the D voters. An incident occurred in Karimganj District as a person namely Repati Das and his wife Tripti Das were suspected as D voters. Although they produced their names in the voters list but in spite of it the BJP general secretary of the State Committee and one of the party member of BJP said that Police Force are used to harass them.

Issues Relating to Defining "Assamese"

The issue of determining the definition of the "Assamese People" triggered an uproarious scene in the Assam Assembly on the budget session of 2015. The Speaker of Assam Assembly Pranab Gogoi recommended, after consultations with 53 different organizations, that the year 1951 would be taken as the cut off period and the National Register of Citizens (NRC), 1951, be taken as the basis for the definition of the "Assamese People" for the purpose of reservation of seats and constitutional safeguards as required by the Assam Accord.[27] The trilogy of sacred existence is haunting Assamese today having sacred identity, sacred culture and sacred land which are the three points of contention that have led to an understanding of an effort to maintain a pure form. Debate that rules now a day in Assam is the preserving the purity and sacredness of being "Assamese".[28] This definition is required to implement the Clause six of the Assam Accord which promises that *"Constitutional, legislative and administrative safeguards, as may be appropriate, shall be provided to protect, preserve and promote the cultural, social and linguistic identity and heritage of the Assamese People."*

The debate has been going on the *"Definition of Assamese"* to implement the clause 6 of Assam Accord which provides the constitutional safeguards for the Assamese people in the socio-political discourse of Assam. The basic concern arises about the identity of an Assamese. The two organizations of Assam namely the Assam Sahitya Sabha and AASU gave three criteria for becoming an Assamese. Dr. Dhrubajyoti Borah, President of the Assam Sahitya Sabha, asserted that, "All people, irrespective of caste, religion, creed, language and ethnic origin, who accept and use Assamese as the first, second or third language will be integral part of Assamese national life".[29] Later these criteria were rejected by various communities like Bodo and others. They rejected by saying that some communities do not speak Assamese as first, second or third language. But it does not mean that they are not Assamese. Hence it can be said that some illegal migrants who speak Assamese will get all the benefits as provided in the Assam Accord. Therefore, they rejected the definition provided by the two organizations. In the search of "Purest Assamese may include most of us in the category of *others"*.[30]

The Asom Jatiyatabadi Yuva Chatra Parishad (AJYCP) has demanded that instead of showing confusion about the definition of an Assamese, the constitutional safeguards for indigenous communities prescribed by the United Nations must be upheld. The AJYCP has alleged the Assam Government is trying to create discord among various communities on the 'Assamese' issue ahead of the 2016 Assembly elections. AJYCP president Manoj Baruah said the defining features of the nomenclature should be finalized keeping in mind about the constitutional safeguards for the indigenous people. Instead of that, he said, the State Government was trying to confuse the different ethnic groups of Assam regarding the definition of Assamese. "The definition of 'indigenous people' should be a universally accepted one. Therefore he added that *"The definition cannot be decided by any individual or an organization"*.[31] On March 17, 2015, AASU and 25 ethnic bodies arrived at a decision that there should be constitutional safeguards and hundred (100) percent seat reservation in local bodies, State Assembly and the Parliament for *Indigenous People*. The twenty six (26) organizations said that this terminology would resolve all the problems arrived because of the Definition of the term Assamese. The transformation of Assamese into Indigenous people is a radical departure from the Assam Accord which helps in the development of the discourse of nationality in the Assam.[32] Even the Bodo Sahitya Sabha (BSS) suggested that instead of *"Assamese"*, the term *"Indigenous"* people should be used to implement the clause 6 of Assam Accord. The General Secretary of BSS namely Kamalakanta Mushahari said on 6th March, 2015 that constitutional safeguard of the indigenous communities of the State is a serious issue and it must be careful that no foreign national can enjoy these safeguards. Further he added that there are many ethnic groups in Assam and their rights must be protected. The *Chalanta Abhidhan* published by Political Department of Government of Assam with Dr. Maheswar Neog as the editor-in-chief defines the term "Assamese" as 'People of Assam, speaking Assamese language, and indigenous languages of Assam'.[33] From the definitions it can be understood that a person speaking Assamese or any other dialect of Assam irrespective of religion, caste, community can be regarded as Assamese.

The Definition of Assamese has nothing to do with the updation of NRC but it is made popular by the Government to delay the process of updation and creating confusion among the people living in the state. Again it is nothing but the interest of Government on the Vote Bank Politics.

Land Swap Deal with Bangladesh and the Role of Different Political Parties

The Land Boundary Agreement between the Government of Bangladesh and Government of India was signed in New Delhi on May 16, 1974. Both countries were able to conclude the Land Boundary Agreement in 1974, soon after the independence of Bangladesh, to find a solution to the complex nature of border demarcation. This Agreement was signed between the Prime Minister of India Mrs. Indira Gandhi and Prime Minister of Bangladesh Sheikh Mujibur Rahman which provided for the exchange of enclaves and the surrender of adverse possessions. In that time the Indian National Congress tried to settle the border-dispute problem, which would arise in the later time. Under the agreement, India received 51 of the 71 enclaves from Bangladesh (from 51 to 54 of the 74 chhits) that are inside India proper (7,110.2 acres, 2,877.4 ha), while Bangladesh received 95 to 101 of the 103 Indian enclaves (111 out of 119 chhits) that are inside Bangladesh proper (17,160.63 acres, 6,944.66 ha). Apparently Bangladesh retained the 4,617 acres (1,868 ha) of its Dahagram-Angarpota enclave. India acquired 2,777.038 acres (1,123.827 ha) adverse possession areas and transferred 2,267.682 acres (917.698 ha) adverse possession areas to Bangladesh. After the exchange enclaves, India lost around 40 km^2 (10,000 acres) to Bangladesh.[34]

The Protocol (referred to as the 2011 Protocol) to the 1974 LBA, signed on 6th September 2011 during the visit of the Prime Minister of India to Bangladesh, paves the way for a settlement of the outstanding land boundary issues between the two countries. This historic agreement will contribute to a stable and peaceful boundary and create an environment conducive to enhanced bilateral cooperation. It will result in better management and coordination of the border and strengthen the ability to deal with smuggling, illegal activities and other trans-border crimes.[35] This protocol was signed under the UPA Government. They wanted to solve the border issues.

After the four decades India and Bangladesh have started the exchange of 162 adversely-held enclaves. It is the beginning of the implementation of their landmark land boundary agreement (LBA). While India will hand over 51 enclaves, comprising 7,110 acres to Bangladesh, the neighboring country will give India 111 enclaves comprising around 17,160 acres. According to an estimate, around 37,000 people are living in Indian enclaves in Bangladesh while 14,000 people are staying in enclaves of Bangladesh in India.[36] According to the LBA of 1974, **Article 3** provides *"The Governments of Bangladesh and India agree that when areas are transferred, the people in these areas shall be given the right of staying on where they are, as national of the State to which the areas are transferred. Pending demarcation of the boundary and exchange of territory by mutual agreement, there should be no disturbance of the status quo and peaceful conditions shall be maintained in the border regions. Necessary instructions in this regard shall be issued to the local authorities on the border by the two countries"*.[37] Therefore people have the right to decide whether they want to stay.

The next initiative was done on the land boundary issue by NDA Government under the Prime Ministership of

Narendra Modi. The land boundary agreement finally passed in the both houses and becomes an Act i.e. The Land Exchange Act through the 119th amendment of the constitution of India. On 1 August, 2015 India and Bangladesh exchanged their lands. The Enclave residents on both sides of the border can have the right to enjoy the benefits of nationality of India or Bangladesh and access civic services, education, health-care and other facilities provided by the two governments to their respective nationals. By Virtue of the Act, about 14,000 people of Bangladesh living here in the Indian enclaves are given the status of Indian Citizenship. On the other hand, India is given up 111 enclaves with 17,670 acres of land to the Bangladesh, which is already there. In there out of 37,000 populations, 1000 are ready to come in India. Therefore the Government of India according to Article 3 of Land Boundary Agreement India is bound to give them the status of Indian Citizenship. The Central Government has released a huge amount that is 3,048 crore to the rehabilitation of the displaced person because of this Act.[38]

But the biggest irony is that the Central Government did not take any step to detect and deport the illegal migrants from Assam to their homeland. With the exchange of the *Land Exchange Act*, people are of believed that the Central Government would sign the Repatriation Treaty with Bangladesh Government with the same kind of seriousness like earlier they did with the land swap deal. The fact is that without any kind of repatriation treaty it is impossible to deport all the illegal migrants despite of their detection. Neither the Congress nor The BJP Government has initiated any treaty with Bangladesh regarding this issue. In Fact the NDA Government now ordered to accept the Hindu Migrants coming from Bangladesh. In the campaigning time and in their election manifesto they promised people to solve this burning issue of Assam, but after getting power the issue left behind them. The Supreme Court directed the Government to increase the number of Foreigners Tribunals at least hundred (100) but at present it is only thirty six (36) which work in a very slow manner. Both the Central and State Government take the responsibility to delete the names of foreigner if included and put them in detention camps till they could be deported after making the repatriation treaty.[39]

After the *Land Exchange Act* is implemented, the clearly demarcated Indo-Bangla boundary should be sealed so that further infiltration can be stopped as well as the trade of banned drugs, movement of terrorists, supply of fake Indian notes, exports of herds of cows to Bangladesh can be stopped too. Number of BSF should be increased. Again according to Article 4 of LBA provides that The Government of Bangladesh and India agree that any dispute concerning the interpretation or implementation of this Agreement shall be settled peacefully through mutual consultations.[40] The acceptance of enclave areas people as Indian Citizens and to accept the Hindu Migrants from Bangladesh is another challenge for the NRC updation process.

Conclusion

In Assam the process of updating NRC is being carried on. The final draft of NRC is published in 31st Aug, 2019. After the updation of NRC India must sign a repatriation treaty with Bangladesh so that after the work is done, those identified as illegal migrants can be deported to their State.

It is found that both the Central Government led by BJP and State Government led by Congress have not taken the dangerous issue of illegal infiltration of foreign nationals from Bangladesh into Assam seriously. Agreements and accords are made from time to time, but these are never implemented.[41] The sheer betrayal of the Governments in this respect has already vexed the minds of the indigenous people of Assam. Apart from this, it is a positive step that under the direct supervision of the Supreme Court, the NRC 1951 is updated. It will not only help in the correction of the Voter's list on the basis of the updated NRC, but also deals with the detection and deportation of illegal infiltrators. In this process of preparing such a vital document, it should be careful to see whether fake documents are not submitted by any people to claim Indian Citizenship.[42] Hence, it can be concluded that though various issues and challenges have come in the way of NRC updation process in the State, but the updation process is carried on in a systematic way.

Endnotes and References

1. http://nrcassam.nic.in/, accessed on 03/09/2019.
2. http://peoplesvoice.in/wp-content/uploads/2015/08/NRC-Updation-in-Assam-Prospects-and-Challenges.pdf, accessed on 16/09/2019.
3. The Assam Tribune, Dibrugarh, June 26, 2015.
4. http://www.assamtribune.com/, accesed on 29/08/2019.
5. http://peoplesvoice.in/wp-content/uploads/2015/08/NRC-Updation-in-Assam-Prospects-and-Challenges.pdf, accessed on 16/09/2019.
6. *Ibid*, p. 4.
7. *Ibid*, p. 5.
8. *Ibid*, p.05.
9. *Ibid*, p. 05.
10. http://peoplesvoice.in/wp-content/uploads/2015/08/NRC-Updation-in-Assam-Prospects-and-Challenges.pdf, accessed on 16/09/2019.
11. http://nrcassam.nic.in/, accessed on 19/09/2019.
12. Report on NRC Updation in Assam: Prospects and Challenges, pp. 7-9.
13. *Ibid.*
14. Pranjit Agarwala's article in The Assam tribune, "Migrants issue and the socio-political harmony", Dibrugarh, Sunday, Oct 11, 2015.
15. The Assam Tribune, Dibrugarh, Sunday, Nov 8, 2015.
16. Artice authored by Manmohan Das, titled as *Assam Accord and NRC update* in The Assam Tribune, Dibrugarh, Monday, Nov 09, 2015.
17. *Ibid.*
18. The Assam Tribune, Dibrugarh, Sep, 12, Saturday, 2015.

19. Nilim Akash Kashyap(2014), *AASU Swapna: Duswapna: Itihaax,* Guwahati: Assam Publishing Company, p. 264.
20. The Assam Tribune, Dibrugarh, Thursday, Sep, 10, 2015.
21. https://online.assam.gov.in/web/homepol, accessed on 17/09/2019.
22. Report on NRC Updation in Assam: Prospects and Challenges, p. 3.
23. *Ibid,* p. 4.
24. *Ibid,* p. 4.
25. https://online.assam.gov.in/web/homepol, accessed on 10/09/2019.
26. Assam Tribune, Dibrugarh, Saturday, June 29, 2015.
27. http://www.thehindu.com/news/national/other-states/assamese-people-definition-rocks-assembly/article7055297.ece accessed on 21/09/2019.
28. Pallavi Deka's article "Being 'Assamese': the trilogy of sacred existence in The Assam Tribune, Monday, June 8, 2015.
29. http://www.assamtribune.com/, accesed on 29/08/2019.
30. http://www.assamtribune.com/, accessed on 05/09/2019.
31. http://bdnews24.com/neighbours/2015/03/23/differences-in-assam-over-definition-of-assamese accessed on 22/09/2019
32. Akhil Ranjan Dutta's article "Constitutional Safeguards: Issues Unresolved", in the Assam Tribune, Dibrugarh, Thursday, April 09, 2015.
33. Amal Kumar Das' article "NRC 1951 and the indigenous stream" in The Assam Tribune, Dibrugarh, Tuesday, May 26, 2015.
34. Land boundary Agreement of India-Bangladesh, 1974.
35. http://www.mea.gov.in/Uploads/PublicationDocs/24529_LBA_MEA_ Booklet_ final.pdf, accessed on 22/09/2019.
36. http://www.hindustantimes.com/india/bangladesh-india-in-historic-land-swap-after-nearly-4-decades/story-gHXVmfal3DFnFdyfObEz1L.html, accessed on 22/09/2019.
37. Land Boundary Agreement, 1974.
38. Manmohan Das' article "Land Swap deal and after" in the Assam Tribune, Dibrugarh, Wednesday, Sep 23, 2015.
39. *Ibid.*
40. Land Boundary Agreement 1974.
41. ManmohanDas'article "Land Swap deal and after" in Assam Tribune, Wednesday, Dibrugarh, Sep 23, 2015.
42. *Ibid.*

Chapter - 2

Environmental Movement in North-East: A Case Study of Pagladia Dam Movement in Assam

— *Geetashree Sarma and Dr. Niranjan Mohapatra*

1.1: Introduction

The Pagladia dam is one of the proposed dams in northeast India to be built near Thalkuchi village in the Nalbari district of Assam. Originating from Bhutan the river Pagladia joins with the river Brahmraputra in Nalbari district of Assam. The proposed dam site is about 26 kilometers from the north of Nalbari town near the Indo-Bhutan international border. The proposed dam area is the habitat of both tribal and non-tribal community. The area is under the jurisdiction of the Bodoland territorial District. There are about 37 villages in the proposed dam area. Among the 37 villages 27 will be entirely submerged under the flood water when the dam will be build. The proposed project will submerged 20 revenue village under Tamulpur circle those are Namcharia, Plokata, Kandulimara, Uparcharia, Charanjangle, Barbhera, Rowmari, Kandona, Kumarpara, Kuhipar, Surubhera, no 2 darrangpar, No 1 Darrangpar, Sirishghutu, Padampar, Katabhari, Ambari, Barkajuli, Doha Angarkata. Another 7 villages under the Musalpur circle are Thalkuchi, Madaltana, Gerua, Uttarpara, Adla, Barikadanga and Simlabari. The population of the dam area is more than one lakhs. The Pagladia dam project is originally conceived in 1968-1969 as a minor flood prevention project but in 1984-85 the Brahmaputra Board undertook the project and gradually project took the form of multipurpose dam project comprising the Pagladia river and its tributaries measuring 23kms long and 26.20 meters high at the expense of rupees six hundred crores. The proposed project will submerged 70 bighas of the land having high agricultural productivity will be totally destroyed and 6000 (six thousand) families with about 1,00,000 (one lakhs) population will be directly evicted.

The movement against Pagladia dam can be seen as the fight against protection of right to the homeland, traditional livelihood of the tribal in the downstream, which will be threatened by the construction of dams and submergence of their home land. Such displacement leading to not only disrupt of their healthy and smooth life but also forced displacement from their traditional habitat. A major reactions and oppositions from people's organizations in the region came up to safeguard the public interest.

1.2: Project Background

The Pagladia river originally came from the Bhutan and the river is famous as " Pagla Baba". Doronga and Motonga another two river joint in Pagladia near the Thalkuchi and therefore the place is popularly called as "Tribenisangam". The bank of the river is the inhabitant of various tribal and non- tribal community people those are basically depend upon the agriculture for their livelihood. During the flood Topsil, Humus are also coming along with the water and mixed with soil which are very much helpful for the farmers. Apart from these, various types of fishes are also found in the river. However, as the name of the river itself implies that, pagla means "Mad" and it sometimes create a heavy flood to the district as well as any movement it can change her course. In the year 1967, a heavy flood was occurred in Nalbari district as a result the government of Assam thought to commission a dam project to solve the problem permanently.[1] The Pagladia dam project was originally planned as a minor flood prevention project commissioning in 1967-71. The estimated cost of the project was ₹ 126 millions based on an investigation conducted by the central works and planning commission. The planning commission of India approved it as a flood controlled project for ₹ 129 million during the year 1971-72. After that during the time of 1984-85 the project was taken by the Brahmaputra Board. The project authority added irrigation to it and it cost was raised by 2877.9 million at 1988-89 prices. The technical advisory committee on irrigation, flood control and multipurpose project of the ministry of water resource development (MOWR) approved the project in 1990 and suggest the addition of hydropower generation and conjunctive use of the surface water to ensure the optimum development of the ground water resources. In the year 1995 finally the technical advisory committee of the (MOWR) on multipurpose river project cleared the project from the techno economic side. Once the project getting an no objection certificate from the Government of Assam the project obtained the clearance from the ministry of environment and forest and raising its estimated cost to ₹ 5409.9 millions at 1999 prices. The public investment board of the government of India accorded its approval at the cost of ₹ 5266.2 millions in march 2000 at a cost of ₹ 5429 millions for implementation by the Brahmaputra Board and they decided to be complete the project by 2007.

The project took the form of multipurpose dam project with the aims of irrigation, flood protection and produced of electricity. The main objectives was to protect the 40,000 hectors of land from flood and erosion covering four revenue circle and total 185 villages irrigation of 54, 160 hectares of land and145 villages in Nalbari district and to produced 3.0 megawatt of electricity.

According to the project plan, the 23 kilometer long and 26 meter high project will submerged 37 village where 27 will be fully affected and others will be partially affected. Since 2001 started to carried out the work by the project authority such as pre construction survey, investigation, studies, design, drawing. Along with these, the government of Assam also started to talking possession 956 ha. of land for Rehabilitation and Resettlement purpose. Gradually they started to construct the project authority office, roads, prepared the technical specifications and tender document. Finally, in the year 2003, the government announced for the acquisition of land from the villagers. The government of Assam prepared to carry out the necessary survey regarding the project such as property assessment of the project affected families for finalizing the Resettlement & Rehabilitation plan as well as land allotment for R&R and project construction.

However, project related activities could not be done due to the resistance from the project-affected people. Various steps have been by the government of Assam along with the honorable minister of Water resource to carry out the project but no headway has been achieved. On 23rd October in 2009, a meeting was held in the conference room of the chief secretary, government of Assam where the Brahmaputra board officials emphasized that it would be ideal if the dam would be constructed at Thalkuchi. As the submerged area falls within in Bhutan, therefore the matter would be going to the government of Bhutan through the ministry of external affairs, government of India. Therefore the Brahmaputra board carried out studies to explored an alternative site in the upstream of Thalkuchi so that the submergence to be within the Indian Territory. But the alternative site is said to be not suitable for dam construction because of the whole reservoir area falls under the Bhabar zone where there is a higher chances of leakage. Apart from this, the population density upto 10 klmtrs of Thalkuchi is such that the displacement of the population due to submergence is not likely to change significantly and as such no apparent benefits will e achieved. As a result, no suitable site is available in the upstream of Thalkuchi. The commissioner of Brahmaputra Board requested the chief secretary of the government of Assam to offer view in the matter and in the later period, the commissioner of the Board requested the secretary of the water resource department of the government of Assam see the matter but the matter is still pending. In the year 2011, a meeting was held in the secretariat of the BTC, where the Brahmaputra Board officials discussed about the matters in details and stressed the need to conduct the zirat survey for ascertaining the actual picture of PAF to prepared a detail plan of Rehabilitation and Resettlement. The authority also given a copy of "National R&R policy, 2007" to the secretary of BTC to initiate the zirat survey of the proposed dam area but the response is still pending. The matter was discussed in the annual meet of Brahmaputra Board in 2011 and decided to temporarily close the offices under the project and accordingly the manpower which are engaged in the project site has been transferred to the other offices of the Brahmaputra Board. After that in the year 2012, the annual meeting of the Board the secretary of the government of Assam referred to the statement made by the honorable chief minister of Assam about one more effort he would like to make with BTC to break the deadlock on Pagladia dam project. However, due to huge financial liabilities involved into the project, the board members decided to close the project temporarily.[2]

1.3: Social and Environmental Impact of Pagladia Dam and People's Response

The main occupation of the people living in the Pagladia dam project area is natural resource based. Most of them are the peasants. The tribals those who are lived in the project area most of them are poor. Their sole occupation is agriculture and they have some traditional practices such as *Jhum* cultivation, traditional way of irrigation from the hill stream etc. In some record, it is shows that they pay a water cess to the Bhutan officials for drawing water from the streams.[3] They use some traditional method to improve the fertility of land. Most of them are self-sufficient in agriculture. Their some another source of income is fishing, animal husbandry etc. It is showed that in every family has cow, goat, pig etc. they go to the local market and sell their home growing vegetables, fish etc. They also collect medicines from the forests. Bodos are those who first introduced silk cloth in Assam from where they get some economic autonomy.

Above-mentioned are some reasons for which the people think that dam will threaten their livelihood as well as socio- environmental impact in their ancestral lands. To know the view of the responder study was conducted in four villages situated near to dam Constructed area are- Thalkuchi, Madaltana, Kumarpara and Simlubari. From the field visit regarding the people's perception on Pagladia dam following issues are found.

1.3.1. Socio Economic Status of the Respondent

Table No. 1.3.1: Respondent Category.

Sl. No.	*Category*	*Respondent number*	*Percentage*	*Total no*
1.	ST	75	62.5%	75
2.	SC	25	20.83%	25
3.	OBC	10	8.33%	10
4.	General	10	8.33%	10
	Total	120	100%	120

Source : Field visit.

From the above table it is found that most of the people of the region are Tribal (Bodo). The table shows that out of 120 respondent 75 (62.5%) belongs to ST category, 20.83% belongs to Sc category, 8.33% belongs to OBC category and another 8.33% belongs to General category. From this table it is found that if the dam will construct by the authority most of the tribal peoples cultivated land submerged under the project and they lost their livelihood.

Table No. 1.3.2: Occupation of the Respondent.

Sl. No.	*Occupation*	*Numbers of respondent*	*Percentage*	*Total no*
1.	Farmer	80	66%	66
2.	Fishing	8	6.66%	8
3.	Daily labour	6	5%	6
4.	Animal husbandry	14	11.66%	14
5.	Business	7	5.83%	7
6.	Job	5	4.16%	5
	Total	120	100%	120

Source: Field Visit.

From the above table we found that 66% population of the region are farmer, 6.66% fisherman, 5% daily labour, 11.66% depends on animal husbandry, 5.83% doing business and 4.16% engaged in jobs. The table reveals that most of the people of the region are farmer. If the dam will constructed within the region which will destroyed their livelihood. People told that if the dam will build more than one lakh people will be displaced from their home as well as lost their cultivable land.

Table No. 1.3.3: Income of the Respondent

Sl. No	*Amount*	*Respondent numbers*	*Percentage*	*Total no*
1.	1000-2000	45	37.5%	45
2.	2000-4000	16	13.33%	16
3.	4000-6000	12	10%	12
4.	6000-8000	15	12.5%	15
5.	8000-10,000	17	14.16%	17
6.	10,000-12,000	10	8.33%	10
7.	More than 12,000	5	4.16%	5

Source: Field Visit

From this table we have seen the income of the people of the region. 37.5% people income between 1000-2000, 13.33% people income between 2000-4000,10% people income between 4000-6000, 12.5% people income between 6000-8000, 14.16% people income between 8000-10,000, 8.33% people income between 10,000-12,000 and only 4.16% people income above 12,000. From the table it can be said that most of the peplewithin the region are poor and if the dam will submerged their land than they will become poorer.

Table No. 1.3.4: Educational Qualification of the Respondent.

Sl. No	Education level	Numbers of respondent	Percentage	Total no
1	Primary level	37	30.83%	40
2	Middle level	24	20%	41
3	High school level	20	16.66%	20
4	Higher secondary level	25	20.83%	15
5	College level	12	10%	4
6	University Level	2	1.66%	2
	Total	120	100	120

Source: Field Visit.

From the table we have seen the education qualification of the respondents. Table reveals that 30.83% people of the region educate up to only primary level and only 1.66% people are educated up to university level which is very low. Table reveals that most of the people of the region are not educated because of poverty.

1.3.2. Impact of Pagladia Dam on Socio Economic Life of the People

The construction of Pagladia dam has influence upon the socio economic life of the people of the region.

Table No. 1.3.2.1: Pagladia Dam Area Land Category.

Sl. No	Category
1.	Public land
2.	Cultivable land
3.	Holy place
4.	Private land

Source: Field Study.

From the table we have seen that project will submerged public land which include school, Libraries, local shop area, Religious institute, cultivable land and Private land which will alienated people from primary facilities as well as destroyed their rights and livelihood.

Table No. 1.3.2.2: Source of Drinking Water.

Sl. No.	*Source of drinking water*	*Number of respondent*	*Percentage*	*Total no*
1.	Running water	10	8.33%	10
2.	River water	81	67.5%	81
3.	Ring Well or other such kinds of sources	29	24.16%	29
	Total	120	100	120

Source: Field Visit.

From the above table it is found that most of the people of the region depends upon the river water. 67.5% people depends on river water, 24.16% people depends on ring well or such other sources and only 8.33% depends on the running water. People told that if the project will build on the river than river water will be polluted which will cause various diseases.

Table No. 1.3.2.3: Dam Will Impact on River Water.

Sl.No.	*Affected area*	*Yes*	*No*	*Total*
1.	Right bank of the river	22	5	22
2.	Left bank of the river	30	3	3
3.	Domestic use of water	55	5	51
	Total	107(89.16%)	13	120

Source Field Study.

From the table it is found that dam will impact on freshwater of the river so far as right bank, left bank or domestic purpose is concerned. 89.16% people told that dam will impact on the fresh river water. People told that there are various species of fish were found in the river, if river water will polluted their species will be extinct from the river. Study also found that many people of the region fishing in the river water for their livelihood that will be destroyed.

Table No. 6.7.4: Dam Will Impact on Fish Destruction.

Sl.No.	Category	Numbers of respondent	Percentage
1.	Yes	98	81.66%
2.	No	22	18.33%
	Total	120	100

Source: Field Visit.

From the table we have seen that dam will impact on the more than thousands of species of fishes livening within the river. 81.66% responder told that dam will impact on the various species of fishes and only 18.33% told not. The river is rich in various species of fishes construction of dam will polluted the river water as well as oxygen level will reduced in the river a result fish will extinct from the river. Many people of the region fishing in the river water for their livelihood which will destroy by the dam.

Table No. 1.3.2.4: Dam Will Impact on Soil.

Sl. No.	Impact area	Yes	No	Total
1.	Right bank of the river	46	10	56
2.	Left bank of the river	34	7	41
3.	Upstream and downstream	14	9	23
	Total	94 (78.33%)	25	120

Source: Field Visit.

From the above table we have seen that the dam will impact on the soil of the region. From the views of the respondent it is found that 78.33% people told that dam will impact on the soil. According to the people most of dam are peasant if dam will construct than their fertile land will destroyed by the project which might be not suitable for cultivation. People also told that the river Pagladia is considered as “Mad” river which may change its course at any time. Construction of dam will impact upon the entire environment including soil, river.

Table -1.3.2.5: Flood Havoc in Assam annually.

Sl. No.	Year	Numbers of affected district	Affected numbers
1.	2014	18	1846
2.	2015	14	10,031
3.	2016	23	2893
4.	2017	15	150 above
5.	2018	9	90,000

Source: www.floodlist.comandwww.m.economictimes.com, http://reliefweb.int/report/india/india-fresh-waves-floods-assam-leaves-3-dead-and-25000-displaced accessed on January 2019.

From the above table we have seen the every year flood havoc in Assam. In every year flood affected the various district of Assam. According to the people of the project area construction of dam might create flood in future because the river Pagladia change its course at any moment, destruct and destroyed. People said that construction of dam will destroyed the river and it will create more flood, they have lots of experience of the local people so far as Pagladia flood is concerned..

1.4. Government Measures Regarding the Movement

With the construction of big dam various movement are going on with the region. There are many civil society organizations that were protests against the Pagladia dam project since its proposal.

Table No. 1.4.1: Government Activities Regarding the Protests.

Sl. No.	Category	Number of respondent	Percentage
1.	Lathi Charged	50	41.66%
2.	Arrest for illegal assembly	25	20.83%
3.	Invite joint session	15	12.55%
4.	Firing	30	25%
	Total	120	100

Source: Field Visits.

From the above table we have seen the government activities on the protesters. 41.66% responder told about the lathi charged upon the protesters, 20.83% responder told that government arrested the protester against illegal assembly, 12.55% told that government invite joint session for negotiate the matter of construction of dam within the region and another 25% told that police firing among the protesters when they were going to stop the project officials to entered into the village for survey.

Table -1.4.2: Satisfaction with the R&R Package.

Sl. No.	*Satisfaction*	*Numbers of respondent*	*Percentage*
1.	Satisfied	108	90%
2.	Dissatisfied	12	10%
	Total	120	100

Source: Field Visit.

From the above table we have seen the satisfaction of the people of the region regarding the government rehabilitation package. 90% people told that they are not satisfied with the compensation package of the Brahmaputra Board. They told that they are not ready to give their land but they are ready to give their blood.

1.5. Conclusion

Pagladia dam project is originally conceived as a minor flood prevention package and when Brahmaputra board taken the project they added irrigation component and gradually it converted as a multipurpose dam project for which numbers of movements were emerged within the region. There are various tribal people are living within the region and they are not satisfied the R&R package of the government and told that it will destroyed their culture and identity as well as break their community tie. Actually the main objectives of the Rehabilitation and Resettlement is base on collective negotiation with the project affected people to make a plan and implementing it as a developmental project to restore pre-project income standard of the affected people. It is not only a simply relocation policy but it also means the improvement of the quality of life by raising their living standard beyond the pre-project level. Generally the resettlement programme of a developmental project include two generations that include protective measures as well as new rights, resources and strategies for the sustainable improvement.[4] It implies the socio-economic re-establishment for displaces. However, in case of Pagladia dam project affected people the project authority had not done any collective negotiations regarding the land acquisition as well as people's perception regarding the R&R package of the project authority. Instead of negotiation the authority constitute some implementing agency with some outsider people to convince the people of the region. Therefore, the villagers not ready to any kinds of compromise with the project authorities and they said that speaking about the resettlement and rehabilitation is meaningless in front of them. Thus the movement against proposed Pagladia dam project was started since its proposal periods and it is considered as one of the strongest and oldest anti-dam movement in the northeastern region.

Chapter - 3

Trans-Border Insurgency in Northeast India: A Study

— ***Bhaswati Sarmah***

Introduction

The region of northeast of India is comprised of eight beautiful states with different terrains ranging from hills to the plain valleys. The entire northeast of India is a home to different flora and fauna and is a popular tourist destination for a number of tourists across the world. Almost all the states of northeast shares international borders with China, Bhutan, Bangladesh, Myanmar, Nepal, Tibet Autonomous Region and is connected with the mainland India through a small corridor and thus became a landlocked region. But the region has also witnessed a different scenario since late 1940s. Ever since the independence of India, this region has been blemished by chaos, separatist movements, mass agitations, ethnic riots resulting in continuous barbaric bloodthirsty events (Bhaumik, 2007).

The northeast India is suffering from many problems starting from lower rate of development, illegal immigration, violation of human rights, terrorist activities and many more. The region has become one of the most unstable and troubled hotbeds for decades. The armed conflicts, terrorist attacks, counter terrorist attacks etc. has been an integral part of the region for many years.

The problem of Insurgency is one important among the others. Insurgency has created uncountable havocs in the entire region of northeast. There are more than thirty armed insurgent groups has been operational in this area (Hussain, 2001).

What is Insurgency?

Insurgency can be stated as a violent revolt which are undertaken against the government. It can be defined as a struggle between a nonruling group and the ruling authority where the nonruling group consciously uses violence (O'Neill, 2005).

The Cambridge English dictionary defines insurgency as "an occasion when a group of people attempt to take control of their country by force". The Merriam Webster dictionary states insurgency as "a condition of revolt against a government that is less than an organized revolution and that is not recognized as belligerency".

Insurgency has been, probably, the most prevalent type of armed conflict since the creation of organised political communities. According to a research, insurgency can be of nine types- *anarchists, egalitarians, traditionalists, pluralists, apocalyptic-utopians, secessionists, reformists, preservationists, and commercialists.* Of these, the first five types are revolutionary as they want to change the existing political system completely (O'Neill, 2005).

The *Anarchists* believe that all authority patterns are unnecessary and illegitimate and therefore the political systems should be destroyed but not replaced. *Egalitarians* try to impose a new system based on distributional equality and centrally controlled structures to mobilize the people and radically transform the social structure within an existing political community. *Traditionalists* try to establish political structures characterized by limited or guided participation and low autonomy with political power in the hands of an autocratic leader supported by economic, military, and clerical elites. The *apocalyptic-utopians* envisage establishing a world order involving divine intervention as the result of an apocalypse caused by their acts of terrorism. *Pluralists* aim to establish a system that highlights the values of individual freedom, liberty and compromise and in which political structures are differentiated and autonomous. The *Secessionists* seek to withdraw from the nation-state of which they are formally a part; the *Reformists* target policies which determine distribution of the economic, psychological and political benefits that society has to offer whereas the *Preservationists* are concerned with maintaining the status quo because of the relative political, economic and social privileges they derive from it. *Commercialist*'s main aim is to acquisition of material resources through seizure and control of political power (O'Neill, 2005).

Insurgency in North-east India

The north-eastern part of India is one of the most unstable areas of South-Asia where the insurgency activities are very frequent. The region has witnessed large scale insurgent activities since 1950s which were directed against the Indian security forces and communities from mainland India (Bhaumik, 2007). The demands of these insurgent groups range from autonomy within the provisions of the Indian Constitution to complete secession and these demands started right after the independence of the country (Kumar, 2018). Insurgency developed in the region as there is lack of democratic space because of special laws which are very draconian in nature and unpopular among the local communities (Bhaumik, 2007).

Soon after the independence of India, the insurgent groups started flourished in northeast. Nagaland, which was a part of Assam, first to witness insurgency movements. The Naga National Council (NNC) under the leadership of Angami Zapu Phizo was first to declare independence from India. The NNC split into different factions and breakaway factions, National Socialist Council of Nagaland (NSCN) was again split into two factions- the IsakMuivah faction (NSCN-IM) and the Khaplang faction (NSCN-K) and these organisations started executing insurgent activities. Similar to Nagaland, the Mizo National Front (MNF) led by the legendry Laldenga of Mizoram started demanding independence from 1966. In Tripura also, from 1970, the militant activities started demanding the restoration of rights of the tribal people which was dominated by the growing Bengali population in the state. In Assam, with the movement started to deport the illegal migrants from the state, the insurgency activities started. The United Liberation Front of Assam (ULFA) was born in 1979. After ULFA a number of other militant groups formed like the National Democratic Front of Bodoland (NDFB), Bodo Liberation Tigers, United People's Democratic Solidarity (UPDS) and the Dima Halim Daogah (Kumar, 2018).

The nature of insurgency has undergone several radical changes in the recent times. The insurgent groups of northeast were confined mainly to the guerrilla warfare against the armed forces, formation of governments in exile, training of the members and camping in the remote areas and involvement in occasional killings. It was after 1995, the insurgent groups were involved in more dreadful crimes including extortion, racketeering, kidnapping, killing of innocents for monetary gains etc. Thus, the shift in the activities of the insurgent groups have victimised almost all the sections of the society including business houses, professionals, companies and all the common people (Bhattacharya, 2012). The insurgent groups of northeast started getting the help from the other countries across the borders and thus the trans-border insurgency has brought uncountable hazards to the entire region.

Trans- Border Insurgency in Northeast India

The northeast shares porous international borders which became one of the major reasons for the trans-border insurgency in the region. Almost 5800 km long border of India is shared by Assam, Tripura, Mizoram,

Meghalaya, Nagaland, Manipur and Arunachal Pradesh with Myanmar and Bangladesh and all these states has been facing trans-border separatist and insurgent challenges over the years (Parthasarathy, 2019).

The development of insurgent groups can be figured out from the tendency of regional states to destabilize rival neighbours by providing assistance to dissenters. The states are the most important source of external support not only in the form of political and moral but also in the form of money, equipment, training and other tangible assistance. The production of military weapons has made the acquisition of external support easier. The insurgent groups may sometimes seem to aim private arms industries for weapons and other equipment. Apart from this, the global transportation and communication revolution like the developments in surface water and air transportation, have facilitated in the growth of external support to the insurgents (O'Neill, 2005).

The external supports that the insurgent groups are getting can be divided into different heads, starting from moral to material. Bard E O'Neill in his book "Insurgency & Terrorism: From Revolution to Apocalypse" has identified four different types of external support that the insurgent groups are getting. These are moral, political, material and sanctuary. *Moral* support includes private and public statements that indicate sympathy for insurgents. *Political* support means active backing for the ultimate goal of the insurgents in the diplomatic and public grounds. *Material* support means all tangible materials given to the insurgent groups. These materials include not only monetary help but also basic necessities like food, clothing, medicine, shelter etc., political, moral, ideological and administrative training. The *Sanctuaries* are the safe heavens provided to the insurgent groups to carry out their training and execute their planning.

The insurgent groups of northeast India enjoyed popular support since they started vehemently protest against the grievances of the people which includes mal governance, alienation, poor development and indifferent treatment by the central government (Kumar, 2018). These insurgent groups are getting support not only from the people of their states but also from the other states in different forms. The strategic location of the northeast along with the access of the disaffected groups to China, Bangladesh, Myanmar, Bhutan and Nepal and with material and moral support of foreign intelligence agencies to these groups, have facilitated insurgency in the northeast region (Datta, n.d). The major sources of external support the insurgent groups are getting can be divided into the following heads (Bhattacharya, 2011):

1. Donation
2. Extortion/tax
3. Kidnapping and demand for ransom
4. Engaging the small but mushrooming groups of insurgents to broaden the tax base
5. Looting of treasury and banks
6. Illegal arms and narcotics trade with border countries
7. Foreign aid
8. Non-governmental organizations – both national and international
9. For the first two sources, the insurgent groups primarily fix on
10. Government officials
11. Siphoning of government developmental funds
12. Business houses and industrialists
13. Companies, contractors and other professionals
14. Politicians.

The insurgent groups of northeast India started to establish the trans-border linkages within ten years of the independence of the country. The chief of Naga National Council (NNC), Angami Zapu Phizo left the Naga

Hills in 1956 to fight for independent Nagaland from abroad. He travelled through the then East Pakistan and Switzerland and arrived at London in 1960 from where he continued to work for independent Naga homeland. After his death in 1990, his daughter Adinno Phizo became the NNC President and succeeded his father for the achievement of their dream. However, the NNC surrendered and agreed to Indian Constitution with the signing of the Shillong Accord in November 11, 1975. But some cadres were against the constitution and eventually they formed the Naga Nationalist Socialist Council of Nagaland (NSCN). The NSCN after its formation inside Myanmar started providing training and other material support to other insurgent outfits like United Liberation Front of Assam (ULFA) (Hussain, 2001).

It was in Yunnan province of China that the cadres of NNC under the leadership of Isac Muivah were imparted with the knowledge of arms and guerrilla warfare tactics and they were also taught Maoism. Apart from NNC, China also provided moral and material assistance to the Mizo and Meiti insurgent groups and impart training to their cadres in Yunnan province and Lhasa of Tibet (Datta, n.d.).

The Pakistani intelligence agency Inter- Services Intelligence (ISI) is believed to helped the militant groups through training and material assistance. It was stated that the arrested and surrendered militants have admitted the fact and several photographic evidences and passports seized from them validated this. However, Pakistan refused to accept the claim. China, on the other hand, was also believed to help the NSCN in 1980s which are not relevant today (Kumar, 2018).

The Mizo National Front (MNF) volunteers with their leader Laldenga went to Pakistan for acquisition of training and arms. After the independence of Mizoram, the MNF were forced to go underground and cross the borders into the Chittagong Hill Tracts and Pakistan started to impart training to Laldenga and his volunteers there. After the formation of Bangladesh in 1971, the Mizo insurgent groups travelled to West Pakistan and developed further ties with Pakistan via Rangoon. The Mizo rebels developed and strengthened their linkages with the Burmese Communist Party and thus managed to reach the Yunnan province through the Kachin passage (Datta, n.d.).

The ULFA cadres later on started getting advance military training from the Kachin Independence Army (KIA) of Myanmar. The ULFA chief and commander-in-chief also visited the KIA headquarters and the Kachin Hills area of Myanmar in order to strengthen alliances with the militant organisations of Myanmar. Later on, the ULFA also started establishing connection with Bangladesh and Pakistan. It was stated that the ULFA leaders have met Afghan Mujahideen leader with the help of ISI agent in Afghanistan. ULFA also set up its bases inside Southern Bhutan, particularly in the district of Samdrup Jhongkar bordering Assam. The Southern Bhutan was chosen by National Democratic Front of Bodoland (NDFB) and Kamatapur Liberation Organisation (KLO) after ULFA as this part of Bhutan was not properly policed, densely wooded and just located in the borders of Assam. Although Bhutan accepted the presence of these militant groups but Bangladesh always denied the fact from the beginning (Hussain, 2001).

According to Indian intelligence reports, the ULFA has established training camps and sanctuaries in the Manas Reserve and other densely forested areas of South Bhutan. The ISI remains the principal backer of ULFA and the ULFA camps at Deothang and Koipani areas of Bhutan and at Chittangong Hill Tracts in Bangladesh have been reactivated through ISI support (Datta, n.d.).

The armed separatist groups of northeast including United Liberation Front of Assam (ULFA), National Socialist Council of Nagaland (NSCN-K), the Kamatapur Liberation Organisation and National Democratic Front of Bodoland (Assam) has recently united under the banner of 'United Liberation Front of Western South Asia'. These insurgent groups worked freely on Bangladesh soil in the days of Begum Khaleda Zia. It was stated that Zia had a close relationship with the Pakistani Intelligence Agency, ISI and allowed the Indian insurgent groups to work in their soil in collaboration with Bangladeshi extremist and terrorist outfits like Jamat-e-Islami and the Jamal-ul-Mujahideen. These groups continued to operate from Myanmar with China's Yunnan Province. Their cadres moved freely along and across Myanmar's border and received support and safe haven in China's Yunnan Province. But they were forced out of their bases of Bangladesh after Sheikh Hasina assumed office. China also provides support and safe haven to the various insurgent groups hailing from Myanmar (Parthasarathy, 2019).

Trans-Border Insurgency and Diverse Threats to North-east India

The Trans-Border insurgency in the northeast India which was started after the formation of different insurgent groups in the entire region, has continued to bring different challenges to the region. Though there were no existing estimates in the pre-1992 period caused by the militants in the northeast region. The Ministry of Home Affairs of India have released a data of militant related violence which have been reported in the 1992-2015 period. According to this data, almost 15,600 people have lost their lives due to militancy related violence but the actual number is believed to be much more. The oil and gas pipelines of oil rich Assam were also targeted by these groups and alleged that India is exploiting the natural resources of the state. The rail line extension project of Tripura was also attacked by the insurgents and these organisations have also hampered the economy of the north-eastern states. The tourism industry of these states has also suffered which could otherwise be flourished (Kumar, 2018).

The trans-border insurgency has also facilitated the emergence of other insurgent groups including Muslim Fundamentalist Militia which was backed by the Pakistani intelligence agency ISI. The northeast region is also facing challenges from the Myanmar based insurgent groups. The Arakan Rohingya Salvation Army (ARSA) of Myanmar is stated to have links with the north-eastern insurgent groups. Already the Rohingya people have fled to nearby Bangladesh and the over population of them leads to the fled of Rohingyas to the adjacent north-eastern states. It is also said by the security experts that the ARSA can also come along with the Rohingyas which can be a threat to the Northeast. ARSA was formerly known as the Harakah al-Yaqin, al-Yaqeen Faith Movement etc. The Indian and Bangladeshi officials have said that ARSA had done terrorist activities in their soils. ("Myanmar: Who are the," 2017).

It is to be noted here that the Bangladeshi envoy commented that the terrorist groups like Jamaat-ul-Mujahideen Bangladesh and Pakistan based Lashkar-e-Taiba has links with ARSA and they could establish links with the Rohingyas which can become a huge security risk for the entire Northeast region. (Laskar, 2017).

Another claim is that at least two Pakistan-based terror groups are working among Rohingya Muslims. According to the security experts, a militant outfit, Aqa Mul Mujahideen, formed by a group of Rohingya Muslims is trained by Laskar-e-Taiba and Jaish-e-Mohammad terrorists.

Also, there is a risk of these militants linking up with the National Socialist Council of Nagaland which is an extremist group of Northeast (Singh, 2017). In a news telecasted on 8th April, 2018 by North-east live channel stated that an alarming proportion of Rohingyas entered India through the Moreh border of Manipur. Earlier two Rohingyas were caught while abducting one girl from Myanmar. After that on February 1, three suspected Rohingya women were caught in Jiribam district of

Manipur and on March 23, three Rohingyas were caught from the Moreh town of Manipur. If these people come together with the insurgent groups then it can bring unpredicted threats to the northeast region.

Conclusion

The northeast India has been facing the menaces of insurgency from the beginning of India as an independent country. The insurgent groups of different states of northeast has been involved in violent activities in order to fulfil their demands which were particularly against the government of India. With the passing time, these insurgent groups have joined their hands with other insurgent and terrorist groups of the bordering countries in order to get advanced military training and to get material assistance to fulfil their demands. Most of the insurgent groups of northeast are backed by the other insurgent and terrorist organisations of the neighbouring countries. Thus, the trans-border insurgency has invited numerous threats to the entire region of northeast for which the civilians and the natural resources of the country has to suffer the most. The trans-border insurgency has also influenced the economy and tourism sector of the region. Although the government of India has launched different operations to combat insurgency problem in the region, yet the insurgent groups are seemed to be successful to continue to their activities with the help of other organisations of the neighbouring countries. If these insurgent groups are continued to work for the fulfilment of their demands, it will carry other unpredicted menaces to the entire region of which the casualties will be higher.

References

Bhattacharya, Rakhee (2011). *Development Disparities in Northeast India*. New Delhi:

Cambridge University Press Pvt Ltd.

Bhaumik, Subir (2007). Insurgencies in India's Northeast: Conflict, Co-option and Change. Retrieved https://scholarspace.manoa.hawaii.edu, accessed on July 2, 2019.

Datta, Sreeradha (n.d.). security of India's Northeast: External Linkages. Retrieved from https://www.idsa-india.org/an-nov-00-8.html, accessed on July 20, 2019.

Hussain, Wasbir (2001). Insurgency in India's Northeast Cross-Border Links and Strategic Alliances. Retrieved from www.satp.org, accessed on May 15, 2019.

Kumar, Sanjay (2018, May 3). The Origins and Causes of Insurgency in Northeast India. Retrieved from https://thegeopolitics.com/the-origins-and-causes-of-insurgency-in northeast-india/, accessed on June 25, 2019.

Laskar, Rezaul H (2017). Rohingya Crisis Can Become Security Concern for India's NE:

Bangladesh Envoy. Retrieved from www.hindustantimes.com, accessed on January 25, 2018.

"Myanmar: Who are the Arakan Rohingya Salvation Army?" (2017, September 05). Retrieved from www.bbc.com, accessed on March 5, 2018.

O'Neill, Bard E (2005). *Insurgency & Terrorism: From Revolution to Apocalypse.* Virginia:

Potoma Books, Inc.

Parthasarathy, G (2019, April 7). New Security Challenges in North-East. Retrieved from https://www.thehindubusinessline.com/opinion/new-security-challenges-in-north east/article 26866778.ece, accessed on June 27, 2019.

Singh, Bikash (2017). Northeast on Alert as Threat of Influx by Rohingya Looms Large. Retrieved from https://m.economictimes.com, accessed on March 5, 2018.

Sinha, Brigadier S.P (2007). *Lost Opportunities: 50 Years of Insurgency in the North-East and India's Response.* New Delhi: Lancer Publishers & Distributors.

Chapter - 4

Globalization- A Paradigm Shift to the Development of North-East India: Myth & Reality

— *Rita Saikia*

Introduction

The concept of globalization has generated a significant place in the International level. Globalization is a system or a process which is growing interconnectedness and interdependence of the human community. Globalization is a complex phenomenon that has had far-reaching effects. Therefore, the term "globalization" has acquired many emotive connotations and become a burning contested issue in current political discourse. At one extreme, globalization is seen as an irresistible and benevolent force for delivering economic prosperity to people throughout the world. Globalization implies that the cumulative scale, scope velocity and depth of contemporary interconnectedness are dissolving the significance of the borders and boundaries that separate the world into its many constituent states or national economic and political spaces. The term 'globalization' appeared for the first time in the second half of twentieth century no other word has meant so many different things to different people and has evoked as much emotions. It has opened the door of many new opportunities as well as formidable challenges. In short Globalization is defined as the progressive movement of goods, services and capital across the world without any restriction. It is interlinked with socio, economic, political and environmental factors promoting open societies, open economies and liberal exchange of goods, ideas and knowledge. With the rise of globalization, the overall qualitative improvement of life and social harmony has to be seen in our society. On the other hand, there are some negative impacts which affect our lives. While everyone welcomes the new opportunities that has emerged one cannot simply leave those negative elements unattended.

India has involved in the process globalization after 1991 and it has played a major role in export led growth, leading to the enlargement of the job market in India. The process of globalization has been an integral part of the recent economic progress made by India. Northeast India is a culturally diverse region of our country. It is a resident of different tribes. Each tribe has their unique way of living and folk life consists of myths, legends, tales, music, oral history, popular beliefs and customs. In the context of the tribes of Northeast India, globalization has already made a significant impact on the life and culture of the people. It is a resident of different tribes. Some of these are- Bodo, Kuki, Mizo, Singpfo, Khasi, Mishing, Deori, Adi, Apatani, Naga, Garo, Nishi, Rengma, Angami, Rabha etc. Each tribe has their rich traditional culture. They are famous for their unique traditional life style. But globalization stands as an effecting factor on the folk life of the Northeastern tribes. This paper is an attempt to analyze the impact of globalization on the folk life of the various tribes of Northeast India. Though globalization brings development to the region but in the context of the tribes of Northeast India, it is predicted that globalization may be harmful for their unique identities.

Profile of the North East India

North East India is the easternmost region of India. It comprises of eight states- Arunachal Pradesh, Assam,

Manipur, Meghalaya, Nagaland, Mizoram, Nagaland, Sikkim and Tripura. North east India region is covering 263,179 sq km which is about 8% of the total geographical area of the country. The region is one of the landlocked regions of South Asia. About 4500 km i.e. 98% of its border is with five different countries of South Asia–Nepal, Bhutan, China, Myanmar and Bangladesh. No other region of the Indian union share common border with so many different countries connecting with the heartland through the tenuous 22 km Siliguri corridor. The States of North East India are officially recognized under the name of North Eastern Council (NEC) which is constituted in 1971 for the development of the region. This region is the home of extraordinarily diverse mixture of ethnic groups having unique social, cultural and economic identity, more similar to their South Asia neighbors than main land India. Geographically the region is rich in minerals and perfectly suitable for horticulture, floriculture and other plantation crops. A variety of fruits like pineapples, banana, orange, lemon, mango, papaya etc. grow abundantly in this region. NE region is famous for most number of orchid varieties in the country. Tea is the major plantation crop grown in here and is the largest producer in the country contributing over 95 % of the total production. The economy of the region is mostly depended on agriculture. The region's high rainfall averaging around 10,000 mm and above creates problems of eco system, high seismic activity and floods.

Concept of Development

Development means "improvement in country's economic and social conditions". More specially, it refers to improvements in way of managing an area's natural and human resources in order to create wealth and improve people's lives. Economic development refers to economic transformation of a region or a country that leads to improvement of economic capabilities of its residents, their well-being and standard of living. Economic development is a movement and a process. Development has a larger meaning than economic growth and it includes economic growth plus change. It is equated with modernization, industrialization and human development.

Globalization and Development in North East India:

Globalization has opened up new and extensive opportunities for worldwide development. Globalization has affected a change across the regions of the world and India is no exception. Globalization is playing an increasingly important role in the development of a country. It can be seen that, globalization has certain advantages such as economic processes, technological developments, political influences, health systems, social and natural environment factors. It has a lot of benefit on our daily life. Globalization has created a new opportunities for developing countries. Such as, technology transfer hold out promise, greater opportunities to access developed countries markets, growth and improved productivity and living standards. Globalization brings some positivity and development to the societies in the following way:

Development of the North-Eastern Society

Globalization is developing our societies. It improves the quality of live and brings high standard of living. Globalization makes the society more modern and comfortable than when it was in the past. It also makes countries become closer. With the invention of the modern technologies people get closer and easier in making friends and getting information. The development of internet makes the globe into a smaller place. Impacts of Globalization on Society can be studied as social globalization. Social globalization refers to human interaction within cultural communities, encompassing topics like family, religion, work and education. Globalization has changed the social settings of societies. It would also develop the social belief and custom of the society. At the same time impact of modernization has to be seen in the society due to the process of globalization. The society of North Eastern India is egalitarian in nature. Tribal society tends to be considerate of humankind, its leadership being based on ties of kinship and temper rather than on hereditary status. The people of North eastern are very much comfortable with the traditional way of livelihood but due to the globalization it has to be seen a change on it. Gender equality is one of the positivity of globalization that brings to the society of North East India. On the one hand globalization has resulted in making the man more interested toward its planet in which he is living and its ecology i.e. its environment through the technological advancements.

Development of the Economic Sector in North-East:

Globalization is primarily an economic process of interaction and integration that's associated with social and cultural aspects. Economic globalization refers the integration of national economies into the international economy through trade, foreign direct investment, capital flows, migration, and the spread of technology. Globalization generally means integrating economy of our nation with the world economy. The aim of globalization is to benefit individual economies around the world by making markets more efficient. The economic changes initiated have had a dramatic effect on the overall growth of the economy. In case of India, after suffering from a huge financial and economic crisis Dr. Manmohan Singh adopted a new economic policy in 1991 also known as Liberalization, Privatization and Globalization (LPG) which was developed a measure to cure the crisis of India. The measures were taken to liberalize and globalize the economy of India. The entire region of the North-East can be broadly divided into two characteristic zones – mountain and plains. The economy of north eastern India is based on agriculture. More than 70% of North Eastern people are engaged in agricultural production. However, the region yet not receives self sufficiency in agriculture. It includes tea industries, sugar industry, grain mill products industry, food processing industry and the textile industry. Apart from it some mineral based industries, forest based industries and the other industries also have to be seen in this region. The economic changes initiated have had a dramatic effect on the overall growth of the economy in the region of North East India. It also heralded the integration of the Indian economy into the global economy. Globalization had its impact on various sectors including Agricultural, Industrial, Financial, Health sector and many others. Globalization creates an international market in North East India and this region is strategically located for foreign and domestic investors to tap the vast contiguous markets of Myanmar, China, Malaysia, Thailand, Singapore, Philippines, Indonesia and other East and South East Asian countries. In the agricultural sector people of North east India used modern technological tools for the growth of the agrarian economy. This region also develops bamboo industries as North East India is rich in Bamboo. Government of India has initiated to development of bamboo industries in NE region. They make pickle, furniture, bags, daily utensils etc. and it capture a huge place in International Market. Because of Globalization there are so many industries like water bottle industries, fried fish industries, potato and banana chips industries, handy craft industry and many more industries has grown up in this region. It would generate employment in North Eastern Region. With this it would also develop the infrastructure of the region.

Development of Cultural Sector in North-East India:

Culture is the characteristics and knowledge of a particular group of people, encompassing language, religion, cuisine, social habits, music and arts. Customs, norms and values are important heritage of culture. The social attitude and behavior of any social group are determined by its culture. North East Indian states are rich in culture and every tribal group of these states has its own unique tribal culture, tribal folk dance and food and crafts. In the contemporary time traditional norms and values are being replaced by the Global culture values and norms. Family is the backbone and basic unit of every society. The traditional system of family was based upon a man, his wife or wives and their children, relatives and there was a good understanding, unity and feeling of oneness among the traditional families but in present times it would be changed into a single family. Language is another feature of Culture and globalization create a global language. With this global language now people can communicate with each other in international level and have a platform where everyone can share their thoughts and feelings. To develop a society language plays a very major role. At the same time globalization also helps to spread the essence of festivals of North East India worldwide. Foreign immigrants and tourists come to visit North East to experience the flavors of varied, glamorous festivals celebrated here which are one of a kind. These festivals get an international concern. Again, North East Indian tribal cuisine is one of the most popular cuisines across the globe. Historically, Indian spices and herbs were one of the most sought after trade commodities. At same time here people are attracted towards the western foods. Pizzas, burgers, Chinese foods and other Western foods have become quite popular. In this way here people get an idea to start new businesses of restaurants on western cuisines. Traditional Indian clothes for women are the saris, suits, etc. and for men, traditional clothes are the dhoti, kurta. Hindu married women also adorned the red bindi and sindur. Again in case of North East Indian tribal dresses, it is very colorful and it is in very high demand among the foreigners. Music is another backbone of the culture of North East India. Globalization brings opportunities for our music to gain worldwide recognition and started fusing Indian music along with the western music is encouraged among musicians. Globalization brings a lot of tourist from across the globe for the sole attraction of the Indian culture or North East Indian culture. This is a big profit for the tourism industry and they willingly make a full fledged effort to preserve the quality of North East Indian culture at its best. The first is the development of a bicultural identity, which means that part of one's identity is rooted in the local culture while another part stems from an awareness of one's relation to the global world. Apart from this globalization brings development to the society and encourage the people to move towards the modernization.

Presently, Globalization is witnessed in literature, music, different cultural elements like dance and drama and even in the way of life. The lifestyle has been shaped under the influence of globalization. In case of youth empowerment, women empowerment, rural development cum empowerment etc. the globalization is beautifully reflected.

The Myth: Globalization and Development in North-East India:

India is a scene of interplay of both modernization and struggles against globalization. On the one hand, it acknowledges the positive sides of India's integration to global economy. However, it also cautions the increasing levels of inequality, poverty and social conflicts and the threat that globalization puts to local and regional identity as a result of overwhelming processes of globalization. Globalization is the process of growing integration of economies and societies around the world. Globalization is not only a tendency any more but also a fact. Globalization has affected a change across the regions of the world and India is no exception. The national economy has become far more integrated with the global economy now. It would make the North East Region more developer than earlier. However, there are large parts of the underdeveloped regions that suffer from prevalent underdevelopment. The north-eastern region is one such region. Globalization is a new concept which enlightens the North Eastern region. Farmers and other small producers need access to global market. In reality globalization is not a new concept and the people of North Eastern region basically feel very comfortable in their local markets than the global markets. The biggest myth about globalization is that it is a process driven by technological progress. It means globalization brings development to the North East region through the technological process. Due to the advance technological process of globalization it would very easy to established peace, harmony and brotherhood in the region. Regarding the political institutions with the help globalization process they would get opportunities to improve the situation through the comparative analysis of other countries political institutions. Tourism is the best sector of North East India which would get most benefit from the globalization. With the help of globalization the North East tourist industry involves in a vast network of business activities relating to attracting, receiving, accommodating, managing and servicing of tourists. These include hotels, restaurants, transport agency and several other related activities. Concerning the concept of "Border" of a nation globalization creates the globe as borderless and with this increasing borderless world, it would established border trade which would not only provide an opportunity to revive the local manufactured units but also serve as a transit corridor for the mainland big industrial units to explore the vast Asian market. This would also bring the centrality and visibility of the otherwise peripheral north eastern region. It is with this vision that 'look east policy' was initiated in 1999. Again so far as culture of North East India is concerned globalization brings a new phenomenon or trends in the culture of North East region. It would create a fusion between the local and western culture and also make an international platform to spread the culture of North East. In case of food due to the globalization North Eastern gets an international flavor in their dishes. Globalization creates an opportunities for the students of North Eastern region in educational sector. It has become convenient for students to move globally in search of better quality education, which has led to the integration of cultures.

The Reality

While there are many benefits to a globalized world or NE region, there are also some truth or corresponding disadvantages. For instance to open up the rich global companies is a very common in globalized world. But this feature of globalized world would not exist. It would push the region into the underdeveloped zone. Globalization creates an International market which seems very positive so far as the concern of the development in NE region. However, the local products would not get that much of popularity in comparison to the western products. The globalization processes have serious implications on the culture of the NE tribal groups. The alienation of the land and other resources which are both their physical provisions and the centre of their culture is an attack on their very identity. Besides, globalization imposes a homogeneous consumerist culture and value system on society. In order to ensure the growth of consumerism, globalization has to depoliticize the minority which gets its benefits, destroy their social conscience and desensitize them to the impoverishment of the majority. It thus combines individualism with a culture where everyone looks after his/her own interests at the cost of others. Globalization helps in the establishment of peace and harmony but in case of North East region it would not work. Insurgency, ethnic conflict and violence of the region yet would not stop. North East India is rich in nature and natural resources. In realities due to the globalization process, environmental degradation has taken place and it would affect the nature of North East region. Again globalization helps in the education sector of North East region but region would not get benefited from this.

Infrastructure and quality of educational Institutions would depict the real picture of educational growth. Globalization would increase the privatization in education. It would create an inequality among the students of rich and poor students. Globalization removes the barriers among the nations and people. But due to the over- dependence on the technology it would weaken the human relationship. At the same time the region has expanded their markets and business with neighboring countries through the increasing concept of borderless but this would also brings the problem of illegal migration, drug trafficking and other illegal works. Again globalization failed in the development of tourism industry of the NE region. It's happened just because of lack of proper policy implementation, lack of awareness, ignorance of local people, insurgency, corruption, and so on.

Conclusion

From the above discussion, here come to the conclusion that globalization can help in the transformation of the North East region into a developed region. We can't say in one word that the globalization creates develop in north east India has been totally myth or reality. Each development mention above can be seen as negative and positive. However, it becomes a point of concern when, an overwhelming impact of globalization can be observed on the Indian culture. The North East region is at the throes of visible crisis. Since 1991, there has been increase in inequality and unemployment, decline in the quality of the governance, rise in smuggling, trafficking, illegal immigration, corruption, reckless of public funds, escalation in insurgency related activities, etc. These have led to underdevelopment and erosion of the capacity of the individual and quality of life. A sense of deprivation has developed particularly among the educated youths of the region. Now, it is time to work on a holistic approach to resolve problems in the region.

References

1. Agnihotri, S.K. and Ray, B. Datta (eds.). Perspective of Security and Development in North East India. New Delhi: Concept Publishing Company, 2005.
2. Pakem, B. (ed.). Insurgency in North-East India. New Delhi: Omsons Publications, 1997.
3. Pakem, B. (ed.). Nationality, Ethnicity and Cultural Identity in North-East India. New Delhi: Omsons, 1990.
4. Chanda, Nayan, What is Globalization? Coming Together: Globalization means reconnecting the human community, http://www.globalenvision.org/library/8/567. 2003.
5. Prabhakra, M. S., Is North-East India Landlocked, Economic and Political Weekly, vo. 39, no. 42, pp.4606-4608, 2004.
6. Roy, Sanjay K., Conflicting Nations in North-East India, Economic and Political Weekly, vol. 40, no. 21, pp. 2176-2182, 2005.
7. Upadhyay, Archana, Terrorism in the North-East: Linkages and Implications, Economic and Political Weekly, vol. 41, no. 48, pp. 4993-4999, 2006.
8. Robertson, R., Globalization, London: Sage Publications, 1992.
9. Verghese, B. G.: "Unfinished Business in the North East: Pointers Towards Restructuring, Reform, Reconciliation and Resurgence", Seventh Kamal Kumari Memorial Lecture, http://www.freeindiamidia.com/economy/19_june_economy.htm.
10. Mohapatra, Dr. Gadadhar., Globalization and Changing Tribal Identity in North East India: Emerging Issues, The Tribal Tribune, Vol-5.

Chapter - 5

Relevance of India's Strategic Partnership with ASEAN-Significance of North-East Region As the Key Area

— ***Jesmine Ahmed***

Introduction

North East India, home to nearly 45 million people and surrounded by 5300 kms of international borders could easily be India's gateway to the east. The Northeast region of India comprising of eight states – Assam, Nagaland, Manipur, Arunachal Pradesh, Mizoram, Tripura and Sikkim that is connected to the Indian mainland by a small 22 kilometre link called Chicken's Neck. Thus, the location of NER is such that it shares only 2% of its border with the Indian whereas 98 percent is surrounded by various neighbouring countries as it shares 1880 km with Bangladesh, 1643 km with Myanmar in the east and south east, 1000 km with China in the east and North East and 110 km with Bhutan in the North and North West and Sikkim shares 97.8 km border with Nepal.

Due to this unique location of the region there are huge geo economic potentials related with North Eastern Region. The Northeast region is endowed with human and a variety of natural resources such as uranium, coal, hydro-power, forests, oil and gas. Gifted with highly fertile land, the Northeast region is the world's largest producer of tea as well. Therefore the states of Northeast India are although small—physically and economically—they are increasingly gaining a significant strategic value due to the territorial frontier of the India's eastward engagement.But history shows that while dealing with the region, geo-political consideration has always dominated over geo-economic consideration. Even after the independence of so many decades, Northeast India remain backward and isolated.

From historical perspectives, only after late 1980s under the Prime Ministership of Rajiv Gandhi, India's relations with Southeast and East Asian countries revived. It is evident from the Annual Report of the Ministry of External Affairs, that before 1985 there were hardly any high level contact between India and ASEAN. Before the adoption of LEP policy, in economic aspects India adopted 'inward oriented' policy. It was due to pursuit of NAM and most East Asian Countries closer to USA, there are limited relations with South East Asian countries on political grounds. But after the collapse of Soviet Union and economic reforms of 1991, there need for regional cooperation with Southeast Asia that provide tremendous opportunities for India.

So when India adopted New Economic Policy at the advent of globalization, India's Look East Policy (LEP)was launched in 1991 by Narashimha Rao Government as a means of development paradigm of new economic reform initiatives in India. It has emerged an important foreign policy initiative that represent its efforts to cultivate extensive economic and strategic relations with Southeast Asian countries which was long neglected during the Cold War period.However, this study is initiated to determine where Northeast India gures in the overall perspective of India's relation with ASEAN.

ASEAN and its Objectives

ASEAN was established on 8 August 1967 in Bangkok by the five original member countries: Indonesia, Malaysia,

Philippines, Singapore, and Thailand. Brunei Darussalam joined on 8 January 1984, Vietnam on 28 July 1995, Laos and Myanmar on 23 July 1997, and Cambodia on 30 April 1999.The aims and purposes of the Association that states in the ASEAN Declaration are:

To accelerate the economic growth, social progress and cultural development in the region through joint endeavors in the spirit of equality and partnership in order to strengthen the foundation for a prosperous and peaceful community of Southeast Asian nations;

To promote regional peace and stability through abiding respect for justice and the rule of law in the relationship among countries in the region and adherence to the principles of the United Nations Charter.

However, in 1995, the ASEAN Heads of State and Government re-affirmed that "Cooperative peace and shared prosperity shall be the fundamental goals of ASEAN." Although ASEAN States cooperate mainly on economic and social issues, the organization has a security function, with a long-discussed program for confidence-building measures and for establishing a nuclear-weapon-free zone in Southeast Asia, with the objective of implementing ASEAN's 1971 Declaration on a Zone of Peace, Freedom and Neutrality (ZOPFAN), and a Southeast Asia Nuclear Weapon-Free Zone (SEANWFZ), which would be a component of ZOPFAN.

Importance of North-Eastern Region

India is a major partner of ASEAN. India actively engages in East Asia Summit and ASEAN Dialogue Forum to enhance trade and cooperation with ASEAN countries. India become a sectoral partner of ASEAN in 1992, dialogue partner and a member of ASEAN Regional Forum (ARF) in 1996; India and ASEAN entered into a summit partnership in 2002 and launched negotiations for a Free Trade Agreement (FTA). However, India's interaction with ASEAN was elevated to the level of a Strategic Partnership in 2012. Significatly, Northeast India can be a pivot in increasing this engagement. Moreover, the strategic position of the northeast is an advantage for the region to become a key player in India's Act East Policy by partnering with ASEAN countries. Northeast India due to its critical geographic location is considered to be the bridge between two sub-regions of Asia-South Asia and Southeast Asia. Apart from this, the region has huge potential for industrial development. Northeast region has a special advantage over other parts of the country in trade with India's eastern neighbours through INDIA-ASEAN Free Trade Agreement (FTA). Significantly, the usual economic and some political gains from a free trade agreement with a trade bloc, the ASEAN FTA was also advocated on the ground that it will promote the growth process in general and development in particular of the North Eastern region of India.

Connecting North-East India to ASEAN Through Act (Look) East Policy

Regional and sub-regional cooperation have emerged as the two influencing factor of international relations and cooperation. So, it is important to recognize that the region's locational advantage and rich resource endowment, including manpower, provides an ideal setting for making Northeast India a central part of the Look (Act) East Policy instead of being a mere gateway. Moreover, the significance of North-East India has grown over the years due to its land linkages with Southeast Asia beginning with Myanmar. The North-East region is not only India's land bridge to Myanmar but also a gateway to Southeast Asia and beyond. However, the initiate of Look East Policy in 1991 by the then prime minister Narasimha Rao was a turning point in this regard. India's Look East Policy started as an economic engagement with mostly ASEAN countries. The proclamation of India's Look (Act) East Policy manifests in that the region's proximity as well as its historical linkages with South East Asian nations would help it to establish strong cultural, social and economic ties. There was a strong possibility that such an integration with South East Asia would transform the region as a hub of international cooperation, trade and investment.

But even after the implementations of LEP, the NER region still remain backward and thus there need to develop more strategy for the upliftment of the region and extended its ties with Asia Pacific. Hence, under the leadership of Modi Government, for emphasising more active role for India specially in the Northeast region, there stressed the need for an Act East Policy was launched at the East Asia Summit in Myanmar in Nov, 2014. This peace policy has got a new dimension as it has shifted from "Look" to "Act". By mainstreaming Northeast in Act East Policy, It should play a major role in India-South East Asia economic partnership and thus help to remove the barriers for the development of the region. Thus, by introducing Act East Policy, Look East Policy turned into a tool for forging economic, strategic and security cooperation driven through North-East India and Southeast Asian. India places ASEAN at the core of its 'Act East Policy'. The Act East Policy recognizes the importance of the North East of India as the gateway of the East countries and it is an extended corridor for growth, progress and prosperity of India thus the development of the North Eastern region is a priority in the policy.

Geographical Connectivity

Due to its geographic position, the richness of resources and the increasing focus on engaging with the east, the region could very well become the new growth mechanism for the country. Act East Policy passing through North East region has now become the centre of geo-economics and geo-politics, positioning North East at the heart of policy. Myanmar occupies an important geostrategic position, as a neighbour, in India's North East. Among ten member countries of ASEAN, North East India shares border only with Myanmar, i.e. 1643 km long border in four north-eastern states namely, Arunachal (520 km), Nagaland (215 km), Manipur (398 km) and Mizoram (510 km) mainly with Myanmar's Sagaing Region and Chin State. So if North East India want to develop connectivity with ASEAN countries, it must go through Myanmar and therefore is a "gateway" to South East Asia. So cooperation and connectivity should be develop between North-East Region and Myanmar. Therefore, recognising the advent of globalisation with the paradigm shift from state centrism to interdependence, the then Minister of External Affairs Pranab Mukherjee illustrates that "Northeast India has enormous potential to explore by taking "geography as opportunity".

Economic Connectivity

Since 1991 in the aftermath of economic liberalization there emerged a positive effect in India-ASEAN relations. Due to its strategic location, North-East India has the possibility to become the hub of business center in South Asia. Trade relations through Moreh town (Manipur), Zowkhathar in Mizoram and Tamu town (Myanmar) have enhanced economic integration to a certain context. India-Myanmar bilateral trade has grown from US$ 994.45 million in 2007-08 to US$ 1.6 billion in 2017-18, an approximate increase of 61 percent as compared to earlier. Border trade take place through Custom Posts at Moreh in Manipur and corresponding to Tamu and Rhi in Myanmar. Prime Minister Narendra Modi at the Assam-Global Investor Summit'18 in Guwahati said that "Act East Policy requires increased people to people contact, trade ties and other relations with countries on India's East, particularly ASEAN countries". As a 'gateway' to South East Asia, among ASEAN member countries Myanmar is vital in terms of economic development for India's North East Region (NER). The border trade with Myanmar already in place since the border trade agreement in 1994, which came in to effect in 1995. In December 2015 two important policy changes were introduced by India – shift from "Barter Trade to Normal Trade" and shift from "Border Trade to Normal Trade". Moreover, free trade agreement is likely to facilitate greater trade integration between the two regions. The Free Trade Agreement (FTA) is likely to remove the restrictions imposed in terms of the number of tradable commodities as per the border trade agreement. As per the agreement, only 22 commodities were fixed for the India – Myanmar border trade. The FTA brings an opportunity for the NER, through which it can increasing the export of bamboo related products. In 2018 budget, 1,300 crores allocated for the restructuring of the "National Bamboo Mission" the people of the North East, especially its farmers. During 2016-2017 India's export and import to Myanmar$1,107.89 million and$ 1,067.25 million respectively. In 2017-18, NER's border trade with its neighbouring countries was US$ 197 million.

Transport and Communication

India's northeast is fundamental to efforts towards regional connectivity with ASEAN countries, given its strategic location. Myanmar, for one, shares a land border with India's northeast, thereby providing a bridge between Indian and Southeast Asian markets. Three routes between Myanmar and Northeast India are identified to be critical in this endeavour: Moreh–Tamu, Zolkawtar–Rhee and Nampong–Pangsu route, which is known as Stilwell Road. Of late, the Government of India has taken up similarly improving maritime connectivity between India and Myanmar is fundamental to their mutual growth and development. So far, the projects that have been undertaken by India with Myanmar include the Kaladan Multimodal Transit Transport Project and the India Myanmar-Thailand Trilateral Highway. The Kaladan Multimodal Transit Transport Project is the first major project undertaken by India in Southeast Asia. It directly link Palewa by road to India state of Mizoram(National Highway 54. India has already completed the rest of the

Kaladan project work in Myanmar. On the Indian side, work is on to extend the Aizawl-Saiha National Highway by 90 km to the international border at Zorinpui. When completed, this project will connect Kolkata with Sittwe port in Myanmar, facilitating the movement of cargo across the India-Myanmar border through the sea route. This project will also provide an alternative transit route between India's northeastern region and Myanmar by establishing new road, and inland water connectivity links between them. There are also plans to connect Paletwa to the India-Myanmar border by road, which will further be extended to Lawngtlai town in Mizoram. Work on this project is expected to be completed by 2020. It is expected to revolutionise the transit system for goods and tradable services between India and Myanmar, later extending to other Southeast Asian nations such as Laos, Cambodia, and Vietnam. The 1,360 km long IMT highway from Moreh in India to Mae-Sot in Thailand can be extended to Vietnam via Laos and Cambodia. Kaladan Multimodal Transport Project is largest and most strategically important Indian investment in Myanmar Also, a 6,000-crore project is under way for four-laning the 300-km highway from Myanmar border to Aizawl to ensure the faster movement of goods. Moreover, Budhi Gandaki Dam – Nepal, Myitsone Dam – Myanmar are a part of increasing connectivity with ASEAN nations. Thus, these projects not only help North-East India but also other parts of the country to prosperity and development.

The UDAN-RCS (Ude Desh Ka Aam Nagrik-Regional Connectivity Scheme), "Let the common citizen of the country fly" is scheme of government of India on regional air connectivity to link Guwahati with all the ASEAN countries. Some recent decisions to enhance connectivity of the North East include a 4,000 km long ring road connecting the states; expediting railway projects connecting all states capitals by 2020, and extending to new destinations; border last-mile rail connectivity with Myanmar and restoring rail connectivity with Bangladesh.

Connectivity is also being upgraded in the border areas for strategic purposes, with highways and development plans approved for Arunachal Pradesh, Nagaland and Manipur, including a four-lane highway between Dimapur and Kohima. Kathmandu Declaration 2018 agreed that the Master Plan on Transport Connectivity would serve as a strategic document that guides actions and promotes synergy among various connectivity frameworks, such as the ASEAN master plan on Connectivity 2025.

Cultural Link

The ASEAN India Vision Statement, 2012 has agreed on cooperation and promotion of greater people-to-people interaction including exchanges in culture, education, youth, sports and human resource development.By cultural connection, India will nourish the growing relationship with ASEAN. Buddhist and Hindu links could be deepening of flowing bonds between peoples. Common ties of Buddhism and culture, a shared history of colonialisation etc. are used in the Act East Policy to build a sense of togetherness. The most positive aspect by which India can project its power abroad is through the projection of its softpower, it is already India massively successful in projecting Yoga abroad. India is home to Buddhism. Many of the countries of ASEAN are heavily influenced by Buddhism. By educating the people of the region about our common cultural heritage we can unify and help form close economic collaboration between North East India and South East Asian nations. North East India has many important Buddhist sites and important monasteries. The path of the Buddha can be traced from Arunachal Pradesh to Myanmar and beyond. India could then utilize the Buddhist heritage circuits, so that there is an increase in the Asian pilgrims annually. In this regard, the festival can be organized that celebrate North East tribes, music, dance, food, art, local culture and religious philosophies, languages, etc. Corresponding, the foreign entities can show how they can contribute positively to the life of the people in the North East States. They are also ethnically, culturally and linguistically distinct, predominantly speaking Sino-Tibetan and Austro-Asiatic languages (around 220 of them), rather than the Indo-Aryan languages of northern India, also with a strong Christian presence.

Conclusion

India's relationship with ASEAN has emerged as a key cornerstone of our foreign policy. This strategic partnership acquired a new momentum with the implementation of Act East Policy as ASEAN lies at the core of this policy. Due to its geographic position, it is believed that the North East could be transformed into an economic corridor connecting India, Myanmar, Bangladesh and ASEAN. Considering long international borders, proximity with the ASEAN countries and its rich resources, the North East has great potential to become a hub of economic activity and trade for India and the sub region. The benefits of such a transformation would be multifaceted, impacting not only India but the entire sub region, and would pave the way for the integration of India's north east with the world economy. Thus, often ignored and overlooked, North-Eastern region is increasingly playing an important strategic role for connecting India to ASEAN member states effectively.

References

Aneja, A, "ASEAN trade corridor could ease regional tension", The Hindu, September 20, 2015.

Chiru Partakson Roman, "Socio-Economic Impact of Act East Policy in Northeastern Region", International Journal of Developmental research, Vol 07, Issue 10, 10 October 2017, pp. 83.

Dr Tridib Chakraborti and Dr Mohor Chakraborty, *Expanding Horizons of South Asia Policy: 'Look', 'Move' and 'Act' East*, (KW Publishers Pvt Ltd), New Delhi, 2018.

Ganguly, Sumit. *'India's Foreign Policy Retrospect and Prospect'*, (Oxford University Press), Thane, pp. 107- 123. 2018.

Gorky Chakraborty, *The Look East Policy and North East India*, (Aakar Books Publication), Delhi, 2014.

Gurudas Das and C. Joshua Thomas, *Look East to Act East Policy: Implications for India's Northeast,* (Routledge India Press), New Delhi, 2016.

H.N. Das, "Preparing the North-East for Look East Policy", *Dialogue,* Vol. 9, No. 1, July-September 2007.

Kadakkadan Fathimath Suhara, *An Introduction to Look East Policy of India,* LAP Lambert Academic Publishing, Germany, 2014.

Partakson Roman Chiru , "Socio-Economic Impact of Act East Policy in North-eastern Region", *International Journal of Developmental research,* Vol. 07, Issue 10, October 2017, pp. 16083-16088. Available on https://www.journalijdr.com/socio-economic-impact-act-east-policy-northeastern-region

Raile Rockey Ziipao. "Look/Act East Policy, Roads and Market, Infrastructure in North East India", Strategic Analysis, Vol. 42, No. 5, 2018: pp. 476-489.

Samir Kumar Das,"India's Look East Policy: Imagining a New Geography of India's Northeast", *India Quaterly: A Journal of International Affairs,* Vol. 66, Issue 4, 2010, pp. 343–358. Available on http://iqq.sagepub.com/content/66/4/343.

Sayantani Sen Mazundar, *Revisioning India's Northeast Through Look East Policy,* Manohar Publishers & Distributors, New Delhi 2018.

Sharma Atul and Swaswati Choudhari, "Mainstreaming the Northeast in India's Look and Act East Policy", Sprigner Varlag, Singapore, 2017, p. 1.

Utpal Kumar De, *Look East Policy and North East India: Achievements and Constraints,* (Concept Publishing Company), New Delhi, 2016.

Wai-Mun Chia, *Jumpstarting South Asia: Revisiting Economic Reforms and Look East Policies,* Oxford University Press, New Delhi, 2018.

Zhengyu Wu, "Classical geopolitics, realism and the balance of power theory", *Journal of Strategic Studies,* Vol. 41. Issue 6, 02.11. 2017, p. 796 available at https://doi.org/10.1080/01402390.2017.1379398 accessed on 25.04.2019

Ziipao Raile Rockey, "Look/Act East Policy, Roads and Market, Infrastructure in North East India", *Strategic Analysis,* Vol. 42, No. 5, 2018, pp. 476-489 available on https://doi.org/10.1080/09700161.2018.1523082.

Chapter - 6

The Rise of BJP in Assam and Its Impact on Regional Politics

— *Tribedi Chutia*

Introduction

After passing through many decades of political confinement, finally, better days have knocked upon the BJP's door in Assam. The unprecedented victory of BJP in 2016 assembly election along with its local ally rang the bell of the decadence of the ruling party, the Indian National Congress and the emergence of a new shift in the regional politics in Assam. Nowadays the lotus is blooming everywhere in Assam except for constituencies dominated by religious minorities. Though Assam is the homeland of diverse linguistic, ethnic, cultural and religious groups, it is well-known for the unity and communal harmony amongst the diversified groups. Despite this, the rise of BJP in Assam is quite astonishing for academia and deserves special attention. The Chapter primarily comprises of four sections. In the first section, it depicts a brief description of the history of the formation, the ups and downs as well as the ideology of the Bharatiya Janata Party. In the second section, the emphasis is entrusted to present a brief overview of the BJP's electoral role in Assam politics till 2016 state assembly election. The third section explains the factor that led to BJP into a landslide victory in the 2014 General election as well as the assembly elections of 2016. Finally, the chapter provides an analysis of how the BJP's emergence is very crucial to the future regional politics in Assam.

Bharatiya Janata Party: A Brief Description

Bharatiya Janata Party (BJP) is one of the major political parties out of eight national political parties as recognised by the Election Commission of India. The others are- Indian National Congress, All India Trinamool Congress, Communist Party of India, Communist Party of India (Marxist), Bahujan Samaj Party, Nationalist Congress Party and National Peoples Party. The party proclaims itself to be the world's largest party in terms of primary membership. Till 2015, BJP had110 million prime members. The central theme of BJP is "Bharat Mata ki Jai". Here, Bharat refers to 'land', 'Mata' refers to heritage and culture, and 'Jai' symbolises people's aspiration. The party believes in cultural nationalism. It indicates the party's intention towards One nation, one language and one culture concept. It has declared integral humanism to be the philosophy of the party which was formulated first by Dinadayal Upadhaya. The centre piece of this philosophy is Antyodaya – the welfare of the last person in the queue.

However, BJP put forward a very critical view about the Nehruvian concept of Secularism and criticises it as pseudo-secularism. Instead, the party talks about '*panthnirapekhsa*' referring equal respect for all religion.

Though the party was formally formed under the name of Bharatiya Janata Party on April 6, 1980, its origin traced back to the foundation of Bharatiya Jana Sangha by Shyama Prashad Mukherjee in1951. Dinadayal Upadhyay took the responsibility of the first general secretary of the Jana Sangha. In 1977, it merged with the Janata Party to contest election against the imposition of emergency by Indira Gandhi. It is important to note that the Janata party was officially formed under the leadership of Jayprakash Narayan in 1977 by merging the then opposition parties such as Congress(o), Swatantra Party, Bharatiya Lok dal and Jana Sangha to defeat Indira Gandhi led Congress(R). The party won a sweeping majority in the 1977 general election and created history by forming first non-congress government in independent modern India. BJS leaders Atal Bihari Vajpayee and Lal Krishna Advani joined the cabinet as the minister of Foreign policy and Information Broadcasting respectively. However, soon internal rivalry and power politics stagnated the Janata party and, finally, in 1980 the Bharatiya Jana Sangha quit the Janta Party on the issue of 'dual membership' and formally formed BJP in 1980. The founding President of BJP was Atal Bihari Bajpayee who later served as the Prime Minister of India in three terms, first for a time of 13 days in 1996, then for a period of 13 months from 1998 to 1999, and finally, for a full term from 1999 to 2004.

The electoral beginning of the BJP as a political party was not impressive. The party contested for the first in the 1984 general election and could manage to get only two seats. However, the decision to support Rama Janmabhumi movement, the controversial Rathyatra of Advani from Somnath, that was supposed to reach Ayudha, the alleged birthplace of Lord Rama and later the incident of the demolition of Babri Masjid made the party very popular within the Hindi heartland. During the period the BJP earned tremendous success to established itself as the prime saviour of Hindu interest in India. Hindutva politics attracted the Hindu voter so profoundly that it became the single largest party in 1996 and maintained its position in 1998 and 1999 consecutively. In 1999, with the help of the ally of the National Democratic Alliance, the BJP formed the government that completed its tenure in 2004. The BJP lost the 2004 general election in the hands of Congress-led United Progressive Alliance. After playing the role of the opposition party for two consecutive terms, BJP obtained unprecedented victory in the 2014 general election with an absolute majority by winning 282 seats under the leadership of Narendra Damodorbhai Modi. Proving all the political speculation wrong the party has also clean swept in the 2019 general election by winning 303 seats singlehandedly and 353 seats on behalf of NDA.

BJP in Assam Before and After 2016

Bharatiya Janata Party contested for the first time in Assam State Legislative Assembly election held in 1985. It entered into Assam politics in a period ofa crucial political transition in which the large part of Assam trumpet regionalism with the loud unanimous tune. The result was as expected. BJP filled nominations for 37 out of total 126 seats. 34 BJP contestants lost their forfeited fund, and none could manage to win a single seat. The vote share secured by BJP was also very negligible. It earned a vote share of 3.56% (Election Commission of India, 1985). However, the 1985 election to the Assam legislative Assembly was very crucial for Assam politics as it was held immediately after the historic Assam Accord of 15th August 1985 (Hazarika, N. 1994). The poll was unique and significant in many respects. It was the first election in which the newly formed regional political party viz. Asom Gana Parishad contested against the decades' long domination of national political party viz. Congress party. It was itself an experiment to understand and measure the immediate public reaction about the Assam Accord. The election also provided a golden opportunity to the leaders of the Assam Movement for establishing electoral recognition on the demands of the six years-long political agitations. The participation of the voter was unprecedented as 79.21% of total electors exercised their voting right (Election Commission of India 1985). Many observers who were basing themselves on past voting patterns of linguistic, religious and caste groups and the presumed reaction of these groups to the Assam movement and the accord feared that the election would only bring about a coalition government and a period of continued political instability(S. Baruah, 1986). But the outcome of the election was pretty unpredictable as it brought about an unprecedented shift to the dominant political trend by bringing up the newly born Asom Gana Parishad into power. This was not only an unprecedented event but also the most welcome and historic event to the people of Assam(Hazarika, 1988). The result of the election also established the influence of another regional political party in Assam, namely "United Minorities Front" which was also a result of the Assam Accord. The party was formed by the Minorities Co-ordination Committee with the support All Assam Minority Students Union to protect and promote the interest and aspiration of the minorities (Hazarika, 1994). It became the third powerful group in the legislature by securing seventeen seats in the election. The victory of Asom Gana Parishad, led by exceptionally young student leaders raised several issues such as "the meaning of regional political parties, the phenomenon of cultural sub-nationalism, the question of citizenship laws and the legacy of partition, and the principles of linguistic states and secularism that lie at the core of Indian political life" (S. Baruah, 1986).

The next assembly election of Assam was held in 1991. The performance of the BJP was comparatively awe-inspiring in this election. BJP contested from 48 constituencies out of which it succeeded to capture ten seats. The vote share also increased up to 6.55% (Election Commission Of India,1991). All the seats occupied by BJP was from Surama Velly of Assam. Niru Hazarika (1994) called the increasing popularity of the party in that particular area as a "new trend in Assam politics". The party also won Silchar and Karimganj constituencies in the 1991 general election. In the Barak valley, the influx of a large number of Bengali Hindu refugees following the partition and the presence of a sizeable Muslim population had created the social base for communal politics long back. However, it was only during the Ram Janmabhoomi movement, which coincided with the anti-Bengali riots in the north-east, that the BJP could gain considerable clout among the Hindu Bengalis in the Barak valley. BJP did not get the support of the Assamese Caste Hindus as early as 1991 as they see BJP only as a Marwari party (Srikanth H, 1999). The influential section of the Assamese society also did not accept the BJP's policy of being soft to the Hindu immigrant and hard on Muslim immigrant.

The most crucial thing in this election was that the outcome showed the quick decadence of the popularity of AGP and UMF as a regional party. AGP enabled to win only 19 out of 121contestents, and UMF failed to secure any seat. On the other hand, Congress party after a break of one consecutive term again back to power by occupying 66 seats with full majority. The failure to deal with the detention and deportation of foreigners speedily, inefficiency in solving the problem of unemployment, industrialisation etc. Massive corruption and factionalism and split in the party might be considered as the major factors of AGP's lose in this election (Srikanth H, 1999). Regarding the victory of Congress in the 1991 election to the legislative assembly of Assam, A K Baruah and Sandhya Goswami (1999) pointed out that the Congress party performed much better in the areas dominated by non-Assamese speaking population. "Out of the 65 seats it captured, at least 40 were constituencies where 'Ana-Asomiya', 'Na- Asomiya' or the tea garden labour population was electorally significant" (A. K. Baruah & Goswami, 1999).

In the state assembly election in 1996, BJP placed their candidatures for 117 constituencies but managed to win only four seats all from Bengali dominated region. However, this time, BJP improved their vote share in the other areas as well. BJP's vote share in this election was 10.41%. The mandate of the result vehemently rejected the authoritarian regime of Hiteswar Saikia of INC and once again imparted trust on the regional party Asom Gana

Parishad. Interestingly, in this election, AGP entered into a pre-polling alliance with the Left parties and also succeeded to gain support from the United People's Party of Assam, a party based on Muslims interest.

However, the real breakthrough for the BJP in the Brahmaputra valley came during the 1998 parliamentary elections, when its election manifesto offered an attractive package to the whole of the north-east. The manifesto expressed serious concern about the dangers of illegal migration and vowed to proceed time bound steps to intercept illegal immigrants and detect the already settled infiltrators and delete their names from the voters' list. It assured to repeal the IM(DT) Act and toughen the existing immigration laws and rules. It spoke of the national register and identity cards for all legal citizens (Srikanth H, 1999). Through these promises, BJP somehow succeeded to convince the Assamese middle-class Hindus, especially in the urban areas that BJP could be the saviour of the Assamese caste Hindu groups from the peril of illegal immigration. In the next parliamentary elections in 1998, although BJP could win only from Silchar, its vote share in the state increased to 24.5 per cent, and in the parliamentary elections in 1989, the vote share of BJP reached about 30 per cent, emerging as the main rival of congress in all constituencies. Significantly, the outcome of the election showed that for the first time BJP proved its influential existence in the Brahmaputra valley by winning the prestigious Guwahati and Nagaon seats.

The 2001s assembly election was significant for both AGP and BJP as both the parties formed an alliance to contest in this election. Being the ruling party, AGP got the major stake, 77 out of 126 constituencies and the central leadership of BJP were seemed to be happy with the 46 seats for contesting in the election. Despite the opposition from the BJP's state leadership the decision taken by the party High Command to make a pre-poll alliance with AGP was proven to be very practical and visionary that moved the politics into a new dimension.

Being the torch bearer of regional politics, the AGP's decision to ally with BJP had provided recognition and legitimacy to the communal agenda of BJP throughout the Assam and more particularly in the upper Assam. It is significant to note that in 1996 assembly election AGP enabled to regain power by allying with the Left parties. The AGP, which won 63 of the total of 126 seats in the May 1996 Assembly elections, was running the government with the support of the Left parties. While the United People's Party of Assam (now the Samajwadi Party), with one MLA, and the Communist Party of India, with three MLAs, had their representatives in the Ministry, two other alliance partners, the Communist Party of India (Marxist) and the Autonomous State Demand Committee (ASDC), supported the government from the outside. The CPI(M) has two seats and the ASDC five in the Assembly. The position of the AGP government led by Prafulla Kumar Mahanta was strengthened when a Bodo formation, the People's Democratic Front (PDF), with five legislators decided to support it (Chaudhuri, 2001). However, the decision to go for an alliance with BJP broke down the tie with the coalition partner that followed the resignation of Flood Control Minister Promode Gogoi of the CPI and the Irrigation Minister Abdul Muhib Majumdar of the Samajwadi Party from the State Cabinet.

In this election, AGP faced a humiliating defeat, managed to win only 20 seats. On the contrary, BJP won 8 seats, gaining four seats from the 1996 assembly election. Congress became victorious and again came back to power by winning 71 seats and continued to rule till 2014 for three consecutive terms under the chief ministership of Tarun Gogoi. However, the unprecedented victory of BJP in the 2014 general election brought a political shift in the Assam politics as in this election BJP won seven seats for the first time out of total 14 seats. In the 2016 state assembly election, BJP formed a coalition with AGP and Bodoland Peoples Front (BPF) to fight against the ruling party Congress who had a pre-poll alliance with the United People's Party (UPP) in the Bodoland Territorial Autonomous Districts (BTAD) region. By making a coalition with the AGP and the BPF, BJP crafted it crafted a new social coalition as well as an electoral alliance along the ethnic axis in Assam based principally upon the precedence of regional subtext (Tripathi, Das, & Goswami, 2018). The BJP led coalition swept in the election with an unprecedented victory. BJP fought on 90 seats and enabled to win in good sixty seats. AGP could increase four seats by winning 14 seats. BPF was seen enabling to maintain the previous tally of 12 seats. All India Democratic front lost four seats reducing its number to 13. The BJP gained 55 seats and 18% vote share, while the Congress lost 52 seats and around 8 percent vote share. The emergence of BJP as the single largest party has signified the beginning of a new era in the Assam politics which would be very crucial for the future of regional politics of Assam.

Rationale Behind the Growth of BJP

The BJP, once nowhere in the electoral politics of Assam, has become the most dominant political force in the region by 2014, which enabled to capture seven out of the fourteen parliamentary seats. Undoubtedly, many factors had to have remarkable contributions that helped BJP to systematically and strategically plant its Hindutva ideology firstly in the Barak Valley and then spread it gradually and consistently into the various corners of Brahmaputra valley.

It has already been pointed out that Assam was not a fertile land for BJP to flourish as the Assamese sub-national identity was not religious-centric, but it is primarily based on culture, ethnicity and language. In the 1980s when BJP was struggling to rescue the forfeited money of its contestants, the newly emerged regional party AGP was widely accepted in the electoral politics of the region as the symbol of aspiration of the Assamese sub-national groups. However, the people of Assam soon felt a sense of betraying by the AGP leaders as they failed to provide a quick solution of any of the burning issues more particularly the matter of detention and deportation of the illegal foreigners. Allegations of massive corruption against the AGP leaders, internal conflict, factionalism further destroyed the image of the party. BJP took full advantage of people's dissatisfaction against AGP and very consciously and strategically began to project itself as the alternative to AGP by appropriating the core demands of AGP. The election manifesto of BJP in 1998 general election reflected such appropriation. During the period of NDA government the central leadership of BJP outside and inside the parliament were seen vocal about the danger of an increasing number of illegal immigrants in Assam and many occasions they were seen expressing interest for the solution of the long-lasting crisis of Assam. In a nutshell, the disillusionment of the committed regional voters with the AGP along with the rampant factionalism and split in the party paved the way to deepening the roots of BJP throughout the Assam in 1990s which soon became the dominant player in 2000's by forming an alliance with AGP, occupied majority of seats in 2014 general election without being aligned with former major ally AGP and finally formed the government in Assam with an unprecedented victory in the legislative assembly election of 2016.

Another significant development that too indirectly helped BJP in finding a foothold in Assam was the constant interference of ULFA in the electoral politics of the region in the 1990s that affected both AGP and Congress. The worst victim was undoubtedly the AGP. Though it was often alleged that the leaders of AGP during its first tenure maintained the cordial relations with the ULFA, their relations deteriorated at the beginning of the 1990s and as a consequence ULFA played a significant role to overthrow AGP from the power in the 1991 assembly election by providing helping hands to Congress to come back to power with sweeping majority (Goswami, 2001).

In contrast, ULFA was seen targeted the Congress in the 1996 election and backed AGP to regain power. However, soon, the separatist group changed their attitude towards the ruling AGP and had given a call to boycott the Loksabha elections of 1998. In this election, the mere targets of the ULFA's were the AGP candidates and workers. It seemed to have left the congress untouched (Goswami, 2001). When both the workers and leaders of AGP and Congress were continuously scared of the possible attack from the ULFA and were continually struggling to satisfy the separatist leaders, the BJP, being a minor party insignificant in the electoral politics was exempted from the nightmare of ULFA. This political atmosphere was favourable for BJP to silently expanded its support base in the region.

One significant reason for the rise of BJP in Assam has been reasonably explained by Malini Bhatachrya (2016), in her article, "Tracing the Emergence and Consolidation of Hindutva in Assam". In this article she has analysed how continuously Sawam Sewak Sangha, the parent body of BJP and other right-wing forces like VHP and BJP's student wing ABVP have been steadily working for decades to deepening the roots Hidutvo ideology in the region. She argues that the Sangh Parivar and BJP have appropriated the Shankardeva, the medieval saint, social reformer and famous cultural icon in Assam and have strategically used Shankardev Brand firstly to attract the mainstream Assamese community and ultimately for the electoral gain. For this purpose, the Sishu Siksha Samiti, RSS primary education wing which was established in 1979 started its first school in the same year on Sankardev's birth anniversary at Ambikagiri Nagar, Guwahati; the school was named, Sankardev Shishu Kunja. The name and the occasion were both carefully chosen to attract a large number of Assamese students. There are 490 such schools across Assam today that operate under the aegis of the Shishu Shiksha Samiti in Assam. Besides the academic curriculum, in these schools, the students are taught to chant Saraswati Vandana, Shanti path and Gayatri Mantra, along with Borgeet and a conscious attempt is being made to place the portrait of Shankardev alongside portraits of RSS luminaries such as Golwalkar and Hedgewar and drawings depicting Bharat Mata (Bhattacharjee, 2016). The RSS has also been continuously projecting Shankardeva as a torchbearer of Hinduism who successfully arrested Christian proselytisation amongst tribal people. It is important to note that the first Sakha of RSS in the Northeast was established in Guwahati on the grounds of Shukreshwar temple, beside the Brahmaputra River on 28 October 1946 by the efforts of Keshav Dev Bawri and Shankarlal Sharma. Since then RSS has been relentlessly spreading Hindutva ideology among the diversified groups in Assam through humanitarian, political and philanthropic work with the help of its affiliate groups. For example, RSS formed Pahari Sewa Sangh in the 1950s to give special attention to the tribal groups in Assam. Another significant RSS affiliate organisation, VHP's Assam wing was established in Guwahati in 1966. This organisation has further broadened the support base of BJP by setting up hostels for tribal students, homoeopathic clinics and dispensaries and arranging doctors for the treatment of people. In this way, RSS and its affiliate groups strategically worked for the achievement of BJP's desired political goal.

Some other significant developments which can be attributed as the immediate factors for the landslide victory of BJP in the 2016 assembly elections are- the sweeping majority of the BJP in the 2014 general election, strong wave of anti-incumbency against the ruling party , the Congres in Assam, factionalism and internal dispute within the Assam Congress leadership, joining of Powerful Congress leader Himanta Biswa Sharma with eight Congress MLA's in BJP, the declaration of Sarbanada Sonowal, a known face of regionalism with tribal identity as the chief ministerial candidate, the political maturity of the BJP's central leadership in forming an alliance with AGP and BPF, the preplanned strategy to stick on regional and local issues rather than Hindutva agenda plank of religious polarization etc.(Tripathi et al., 2018), (Dutta, 2017), (Misra, 2016).

Assam Gana Parishad (AGP) the Worst Victim

AGP can be described as the worst victim of BJP's gain. The analysis of the political journey of the saffron party into the electoral politics of Assam reveals that BJP enabled to find a foothold in the Brahmaputra valley primarily at the cost of AGP's eroding credibility in the region. It is noteworthy to mention that AGP since its emergence sought to maintain a secular identity of the party and repeatedly denounced BJP as a communal party. The AGP did not join in the NDA government for the same reason. However, the decision to ally with BJP in 2001 state assembly election was turned out to be political suicide for AGP. With this alliance, AGP lost the support from the former partners of left parties and Muslim groups. The alliance communalised the secular identity of the AGP for forever as it impinged an indelible negative impression among the Muslims towards the party's ideology. The result was that AGP's support base in the Brahmaputra had been seen eroding day by day and it is being observed that BJP has occupied AGP's space in the Brahmaputra valley and strengthened its own base in those areas where AGP once had enjoyed predominance. The analysis of the result of 2004, 2009 and 2014 General Election has revealed how BJP had broadened its support base in the Brahmputra valley at the cost of shrinking the AGP's traditional support base in the region. AGP had a stronghold in the Loksabha constituencies of the upper Assam, namely Lakhimpur and Dibrugarh. In 2004 General election AGP decided to contest without forging ties with BJP and secured Lakhimpur and Dibrugarh seats.

Similarly, in Dhubri, Barpeta and Kaliabor constituencies, where Muslim votes used to play a

Table-1

Constituency Name	Party Name	Vote secured in 2004	Position	Vote secured in 2009 (AGP+BJP)	position	Vote secured in 2014	Position	AGP's loss between 2004-2014
Lakhimpur	AGP	300865	Won	307758	Second	81753	Third	219112
	BJP	169123	Third	------	------	612543	Won	
Dibrugarh	AGP	220944	Won	324020	Second	45710	Third	175234
	BJP	202390	Second	------	------	494364	Won	
Tezpur	AGP	219402	Second	352246	Won	40489	Fourth	178913
	BJP	164662	Third			446511	Won	
Kaliabar	AGP	234695	Second	282687	Second	78132	Fourth	156563
	BJP	(No Candidate)	——	——	——	349441	Second	
Dhuburi	AGP	259966	Second	No candidate	——	9897	Sixth	250069
	BJP	90215	Third		——	298985	Third	
Barpeta	AGP	198847	Second	291708	Second	73733	fourth	125114
	BJP	111058	Third	--------	-----	352361	Second	

Source: Election Commission of India.

determining role, AGP performed well and secured second position in the respective constituencies. However in 2009 general election when AGP again went for an alliance with BJP the result showed that this time AGP lost both the Lakhimpur and Dibrugarh constituencies, but, somehow managed to maintain self-dignity by winning the Tezpur seat. The electoral significance of the AGP had eroded to that extent that BJP refused to make a tie with AGP in the 2014 general election and filled candidature in all the constituencies of Brahmaputra valley. In this election, BJP won Lakhimpur, Dibrugarh and Tezpur constituency with huge margin wherein AGP could not even secure second position in these respective seats. It indicates the wiping out of AGP from its traditional foothold. The position of AGP in the minority-dominated constituencies was horrific. In Dhubri, AGP's place was in Sixth while it managed to keep fourth position in Barpeta. Such poor performance of AGP in the minority-dominated constituencies reflects how much the ties with the communal party has destroyed the secular character of this regional group.

BJP has seized everything from the AGP to establish and broaden party's support base and finally to form government in the region. The party once sidelined as a Marwari party by the mainstream Assamese voter gradually succeeded in getting acceptance from them through strategically appropriated the core political agendas of AGP. In short, BJP took over the core regional demands such as detention and deportation of the illegal foreigner, constitutional security to the indigenous groups etc. from AGP and reappropriated for electoral gain. Taking benefit from the AGP's political stagnation and rampant factionalism BJP began to roll out the red carpet welcome to the AGP leaders who sought to join the party. The joining of Sarbananda Sonowal, the potential future successor of AGP in BJP was a big set back for the regional party as it demoralised the ground-level party workers and the committed voters. After him, many senior leaders prominently, Chandramohan Patowary, Atul Bora (senior), Padma Hazarika, Nabo Doley joined BJP before the 2016 legislative assembly election to the state. The strategy of accommodating the efficient regional leaders in the party made the AGP leaderless that posed a serious threat to the party's existence. After 15 years of political confinement AGP is getting opportunity to be a part of the ruling government since 2016. It has brought a ray of hope to the party workers. However, the dubious party stand on the issue of Citizen Amendment Bill, the complete failure in the 2019 Loksabha election has again raised questions to the credibility of the party.

References

Baruah, A. K., & Goswami, S. (1999). Identities Politics in a Multi-Ethnic State. *Economic and Political Weekly, 34*(34/35), 2492–2501.

Baruah, S. (1986). Lessons of Assam. *Economic and Political Weekly, 21*(7), 282–284.

Bhattacharjee, M. (2016). Tracing the emergence and consolidation of Hindutva in Assam. *Economic and Political Weekly, 51*(16), 80–87.

Chaudhuri, K. (2001). An alliance of convenience. *Frontline, 18*(8). Retrieved from https://frontline.thehindu.com/static/html/fl1808/18080370.htm

Dutta, A. R. (2017). BJP's Electoral Victory in Assam, 2016: Co-opting the Khilonjiyas. *Social Change, 47*(1), 108–124. https://doi.org/10.1177/0049085716683114

Goswami, S. (2001). Changing Electoral Trends. *Economic and Political Weekly, 23*(44), 2244. https://doi.org/10.2307/4416969

Hazarika, N. (1988). Asom Gana Parishad. *Indian Political Science Association, 49*(1), 95–104.

Hazarika, N. (1994). Politics in Assam. *The Indian Journal of Political Science, 55*(3), 211–220.

Misra, U. (2016). Victory for identity politics, not Hindutva in Assam. *Economic and Political Weekly, 51*(22), 20–23.

Srikanth H. (1999). Communalising Assam/: AGP's Loss Is BJP's Gain. *Economic and Political Weekly, 34*(49), 3412–3414.

Tripathi, V., Das, T., & Goswami, S. (2018). National Narrative and Regional Subtext: Understanding the Rise of BJP in Assam. *Studies in Indian Politics, 6*(1), 60–70. https://doi.org/10.1177/2321023018762676

Chapter - 7

Untouchability: Does it Exists in the Assamese Society

— Kakali Das

Introduction

The paper makes an attempt to identify the pattern of interaction between the upper caste and the lower caste people. Although the terms 'upper caste' and 'lower caste' are no longer used to describe the categories of people, we may use the terms 'General caste' and 'Scheduled caste' in its place.

The sociologists like Betellie points out that there exists too many cultural differences between these two groups which have resulted in the gap.[1] The origin of untouchability is still unknown. The sociologists and historians have given various reasons for the growth of caste and the rigidity surrounding it. The *Varnashrama Dharma* carried occupational attributes, based on which every caste was assigned an occupation. The groups which belonged to the upper strata of the social ladder were assigned the jobs such as priesthood or jobs that carried a superior status in the society.[2] Whereas the people who belonged to the lowest strata of the social ladder were assigned jobs like scavenging and leather work.[3]

Historical Background

The system that grew out of occupation soon became a system based on birth. The caste boundaries became rigid and with the passage of time numerous sub castes emerged resulting in the complex system.

While referring to untouchability not only as a basic and unique feature of the Hindu social structure, but also as an essential part of it, *The Report of the Committee on Untouchability, Economic and Educational Development of the Scheduled Castes and Connected Documents 1969,* defines the caste system as a sacred institution of the Hindu society.[4] In fact, the Report is of the opinion that any attempt to remove untouchability would prove futile without striking at its root, the caste system, of which untouchability is a direct offshoot.

Clause (24) of Article 366 of the Constitution defines an untouchable as a member of the scheduled caste community, including all other persons who by custom or usage are regarded as untouchables by any community or section thereof. The issue of removing the disabilities imposed on certain sections of the society started much before the colonial rule. As early as in 1858, the Government of Bombay acting on a complaint lodged by a *Mahar* boy, declared that "all schools maintained at the sole cost of Government, shall be open to all classes of its subjects without distinction." [5]

In 1923, the Government of Bombay once again declared that no grants would be paid to Government-aided schools which refused admission to children belonging to the depressed classes.[6] Similarly, in the year 1925, the Madras Legislative Council introduced a Bill providing equal opportunity to all classes and castes in matters relating to access of public roads, streets or pathways. B. R. Ambedkar, in 1928, organized a Satyagraha movement to establish the civil rights of the depressed classes.[7] By 1930, Dr. Ambedkar organized a temple Satyagraha at Kala Ram in Nasik, which was followed by another Satyagraha known as Mukhed Satyagraha in 1932.

Further, in 1936 the Maharajah of Travancore issued a proclamation ordering that there should be no restriction on any Hindu by birth or religion, on entering places of worship controlled by the Maharajah or his Government. Apart from Dr. B .R .Ambedkar, others who took interest in the removal of untouchability attached to the scheduled castes communities, mention may be made of Dr. C.P. Ramaswami Aiyyar, the Dewan of Travancore, Pothi Sri Ramamulu of Andhra Pradesh and E.V. Ramaswami Naicker.

The Government of India introduced *The Untouchability (offences) Bill 1954 (no.14 of 1954)* which was given a final shape in the form of the *Untouchability (offences) Act, 1955.* This Act was passed by Parliament on May 2, 1955, receiving the assent of the President on May 8, 1955. The Act further amended and renamed as the Protection of Civil Rights Act of 1976, was designed to prevent all forms of discrimination against the scheduled caste population. As per the provisions of this Act any offence committed under the purview of this Act can lead to his /her arrest.

Untouchability and its Practices

Unfortunately, though untouchability has been abolished by law, the present study indicates the continuance of the presence of untouchability, particularly in rural areas and in matters relating to the exchange of water and food.[8] The book entitled, *Untouchability in Rural India,* which deals with a survey conducted in 565 villages across 11 states, demonstrates that untouchability is not only practiced in the rural society but that it has also adapted itself to the new socio-economic factors of the present times.[9]

Untouchability is the extreme and the most vicious aspect of the caste system which imposes severe restrictions on people belonging to certain castes and communities.[10] The institution of untouchability implies not only avoiding physical contact but also restrictions on social mobility. According to Dr. B.R. Ambedkar the caste system is a system of graded inequality, the concept of untouchability being its fundamental feature. Social norms considered as the practice of untouchability include the following practices:

(a) Denial of access to temples/places of public worship.

(b) Denial of access to teashops, hotels, restaurants.

(c) Denial of access to drinking water resources.

(d) Denial of the services of a barber.

(e) Denial of services by the *dhobi.*

(f) Denial of participation in social ceremonies.

(g) Denial of access to village *chaupal* (meeting place or gram *sabha*).

(h) Discrimination in educational institutions and public health centres.

(i) Discrimination in the use of utensils kept in public hotels and restaurants.

(j) Engaging the members of the community in forceful occupations like removal of carcasses and sweeping.

(k) Debarring them from engaging in certain occupations like trade or business.

(l) Preventing the use of public cremation/burial grounds.

(m) Denial of use of public passages, roads etc.

(n) Use of abusive or insulting language.

(o) Debarring them from constructing or acquiring any residential premises.

(p) Denial of access to *dharmasalas, sarais.*

(q) Denial of use of jewellery and ornaments.

(r) Non supply of goods from general shops[11]

Untouchability in A Rural Society

The practice of untouchability was prevalent in Assam, though several scholars writing on the subject deny its existence. Dambarudhar Nath, in his book *Satra, Society and Culture-Pitambor Goswami and History of Garamur Satra,* writes that during the period of the Ahom rule it was a practice to tattoo symbols of a fish and broom on the forehead of a *Dom* and *Hari* respectively, signifying their occupation.[12]

Within the three villages of Azara, Palashbari and Hajo which have been selected for the purpose of the present study, the existence of the practice of untouchability amongst the scheduled caste population was clearly evident during the surveys conducted in the area. While visiting the villages of Keotpara and Hirapara in Azara mainly inhabited by people belonging to the *Kaibarta* and *Hira* communities respectively, the people claimed that the practice of untouchability and the existence of taboos related to their castes were non-existent.[13]

At Palashbari, it was possible to conduct a survey only in the two villages of Monpur and Parlli mainly due to the vast geographical extent of the district. Approximately 600 scheduled caste families estimated to be living in these villages and mainly belonging to the *Namasudra* community are of the opinion that they were brought here to ward off an epidemic.[14]

According to popular folklore amongst the villagers, it is believed that it was the auspicious presence of the *Namasudras* that compelled the evil to flee, following which they continued to live in these villages. However, it was observed that the people of the general castes like the *Gohains* and the *Goswamis* living in the periphery of the villages, preferred not to interact with these people considered untouchables, during social functions.[15]

A different version of the story was found amongst the scheduled caste population who believe that there exists no such taboo and insist that even inter-dining prevails. According to this group, the food cooked in a particular a *Naamghar* by the cook who happened to be a high caste person, is eaten by one and all.[16]

Hajo can also boast of a long history of struggle against the caste system. Historical evidence proves that members of the *Namasudra* and *Kaibarta* communities were debarred from entering the premises of the *Hayagriva Madhab* temple. The scheduled caste population inhabiting the two villages of Kaibartola and Majorsupa in Hajo amongst whom interviews were conducted for the purpose of the survey, believe that even today people of the higher castes are hesitant to enter the villages inhabited by the scheduled caste population considered to be uncivilized and dirty. This is more noticeable in the context of residential places and places of worship.[17]

Deprivation and poverty, closely linked with the issues of caste and untouchability, may be considered as the primary causes for the backward condition of scheduled caste women, which differ from that of women belonging to other castes.[18] Scheduled caste women who had been denied equal rights in the past, continue to confront similar situations even today in certain spheres of activities.

Andre Beteille has observed that, “the people belonging to the same caste live together, no matter they are rich or poor or low in other sense”.[19] It actually reflects the morphology of the villages where people of same castes resided together. This is also true in case of the scheduled caste communities who have often confessed about their preference to stay segregated.[20] This is an indication that religion, clan ties and the caste system play an important role in the internal morphology of a village.[21]

As mentioned by R.B. Mandal in his book, *Introduction to Rural Settlement,* that every *tola* was separated by wider lanes, a similar characteristic was witnessed in the villages within the purview of the study.

Although it is believed that the rigidity of the caste system is less in Assam, it was evident during the course of the survey that people from the general caste refused to par take a meal in a scheduled caste household, thus bringing into focus the presence of restrictions on inter-dining, an important feature of untouchability. During the course of an interview, a teacher from Hajo unhesitatingly spoke about the restrictions that existed in his own household about taking food in a scheduled caste home.[22]

In another interview with a lady from a general caste, she admitted about avoiding a meal in a schedule caste household. She was also of the opinion that people belonging to the schedule castes are unaware about matters relating to health and hygiene.[23] The statements made above reveal the fact that untouchability, though legally abolished, is still inherently practiced in the rural society.

Various Aspects of Untouchability

Untouchability also encompasses within it hierarchy, restrictions on inter-marriage and inter-dining. Hierarchy exists as a system of social stratification and is often overlooked as one of the central features of the system while discussing the casual system. Though the sub-division of main castes into numerous sub-castes is itself an indication of the hierarchical status of the castes, in every region there appears to be a variation in caste ranking. However, in Assam hierarchy is also visible in case of marriage.

Kaibartas is one of the largest scheduled caste groups taken into account while surveying into the villages. They classify themselves as different from the *Doms*. *Doms are* one of the early inhabitants of Assam professing the occupations of fishing and selling, boating, lime-making and selling. *Dom* was considered a derogatory term and therefore this group of scheduled caste population demanded to replace the name *Dom* by the term *Kaibarta*.

On the other hand, the *Charals / Chandalas* lived outside the Aryan cultural influence till the early 19th century gradually entered the *Sudra* category under the new name *Namasudras*.

Audrey Cantlie while analyzing the Assamese culture stresses that endogamy is the most preferred form of marriage. The informants who have been quoted in the work say that, there is objection to marrying into a higher caste as well as into a lower; a good marriage is in one's own caste.[24]

Marriage is an integral part of the field of kinship is a public expression that legitimatizes the transfer of woman from one minimal lineage to another. There is hardly any society that does not restrict marriage relations by some kind of exogamic or endogamic norms.[25]

The fundamental reason for intra-caste marriage is perhaps related to maintaining purity of the caste or alliance/acquaintance with similar traditions.[26] It is therefore felt that the practice of endogamy perhaps creates a wall which in turn protects the caste community. Some have even referred to endogamy as a strategic practice to ensure the survival of the caste system. It was Jyotiba Phule's works which have specifically dealt with the violence and gender exploitation as an important aspect in the history of Dalit and non- Brahmin communities.

The focus of the study was transferred from hierarchy to inter-caste marriages in order to prove that the hierarchical status is important while selecting a mate in marriage. The institution of intra-caste marriage is therefore, important even amongst the scheduled caste communities. The current survey also reveals that though scheduled caste communities prefer marriages within their own caste, daughter–in-laws have also been accepted from scheduled tribes, other backward classes and general castes.

Inter communal marriages or a marriage between a Hindu scheduled caste and a Muslim is strictly prohibited amongst scheduled castes communities. Girls from the scheduled castes communities who did enter into such marriage relationships were ostracized from the *Namasudras.*[27] Interestingly enough these groups never intermarried with each other.

There is a tendency among the castes to prefer endogamy. The scheduled caste communities also preferred endogamy. While conducting interview with the elderly women, it was found that they preferred marriage within own castes. Although the social norms are changing rapidly, the scheduled caste still preferred marriage within their castes. Earlier the couple who did an inter caste marriage was ostracized from the society. However, there are certain instances of scheduled caste men marrying women from other castes. In states like Rajasthan, Goa, Gujarat, Haryana ₹ 50,000 or above is provided for inter-caste marriage as an incentive. Assam also provides ₹ 10,000, however the state of Assam was placed with states with no information. The Survey did not lead us to any such couple who received incentive for inter-caste marriages.

Though in reality inter-caste and inter-communal marriages were not accepted in a scheduled caste community, when the question of a girl selecting her own marriage partner was put before the respondents, the survey revealed that the girls affirmed that they were given full independence in case of their marriage. However, the researcher realized through observation that the girls were married off at an early age in most cases without consent.

In case of inter-dining, the various groups within the scheduled caste communities do not prefer to inter- dine. Every caste, in its quest for maintaining its unity, faces the problem of maintaining its boundaries.[28] Out of the mechanisms of maintaining caste boundaries- the prohibition on exchange of water and food (called *roti vyavahar* in northern and western India) between castes, even between the former untouchables and the other comes the first. In Assam, the word 'untouchable' is not used but untouchability still exists in the rural areas.

The idea of inter-dining is still a taboo in the rural areas. The survey revealed how an educated man prefer to eat outside with the members of different communities, but also reported that such instances rarely take place in his home as his mother is still alive. The person reported that his mother prefers to maintain the caste boundaries by not dining with the members of other communities.

Results and Conclusion

These instances come to light while analyzing the prevalence of untouchability in Assam.

- There is a prevalence of untouchability in the matter of inter-dining. The General caste people preferred not to inter-dine with the scheduled caste communities. Even the people from Other Backward Classes accept that inter-ding with the members of other castes is not accepted by the elders of their family.
- The scheduled caste communities in the areas taken into consideration while surveying claimed that the practice of untouchability is non-existent .The main reason behind this is perhaps the scheduled caste people's effort to depict a picture of social fluidity.
- The Scheduled caste communities prefer intra-caste marriages. Although there are few instances of inter- caste marriage .Inter-communal marriages are strictly prohibited in scheduled caste communities.
- The scheduled caste communities have their own places of worship, this is indicative of the prevalence of untouchability that might have restricted their movement into the temples/places of worship built

and maintained by the members of so called Upper castes groups.

Therefore, it can be concluded that untouchability exists in the Assamese rural society, however the caste boundaries become flexible in an urban society.

Bibliography

Journals

(a) Chakravarti ,Uma ,*Conceptualizing Brahmanical Patriarchy in Early India: gender, caste, class and state,* EPW, Vol. 28, No. 4,1993, http://www.jstor.org/stable/4399556

(b) Chandidas, R, *How close to Equality are Scheduled castes*? EPW, Vol. No. 24, 1969, http://www.jstor.org/stable/40739736

(c) Chekki, Dan .A, Social Stratification and Trends of Social Mobility in Modern India, Sociologus, New Series,Vol. 20, No. 2,1970, http://www.jstor.org/stable/4364445

(d) Gupta, D ,*Continuous Hierarchies and Discrete castes,* EPW, Vol. 19, No. 46, 1984, http://www.jstor.org/stable/4373768

(e) Kalpagam, V, *Marraige Norms, Choice and Aspirations of Rural Women,* Economic and Political Weekly, Vol. 43, No. 21, May, 2008, http://www.jstor.org/stable/402277497

(f) Shah, A.M, *Caste in the 21st century :From system to Elements,* EPW, Vol. 42, No. 44, 2007, http://www.jstor.org/stable/40276753

(g) Sharma, Arvind and Converse , Hyla .S, *An ancient account of the origin of caste,* Journal of the American Oriental society, Vol. 114, No. 4, 1994, http://www.jstor.org/stable/606171

(h) Sharma, S. S, *Untouchability, a Myth or Reality: A study of interact ion between Scheduled caste and Brahmins in a Western U.P village,* Sociological Bulletin, Vol. 35, No. 1, March, 1986. pp. 68-79.

Books

(a) Allen, B.C, *Census of Assam 1901 vol-I,* New Delhi, Manas Publications, reprinted 1984.

(b) Ambedkar, B.R, *Annihilation of Caste,* http://www.bapuculturaltours.org/i%20nostri%20e-books/annihilation%20of%20caste%20B00O7GHRYK_ EBOK_2.pdf

(c) Bayly, *Susan, Caste ,Society and politics in India from the 18th century to the Modern age,* New Delhi, Cambridge University press, 2005.

(d) Beteille, Andre, *Caste, Class and power changing patterns of stratification in a Tanjore Village,* New Delhi, OUP, 1996.

(e) Beteille, Andre, *The Andre Beteille omnibus,* New Delhi, OUP, 2011.

(f) Bhadra, Ranajit. K, *Caste and class: Social stratification in Assam,* New Delhi, Hindustan Publishing House, 1991.

(g) Dirks, B. Nicholas, *Caste of Mind: Colonialism and the making of Modern India,* New Delhi, Permanent Black, 2001.

(h) Dube, Ishita. B(ed), *Themes in Indian History :Caste in History,* Oxford University Press, New Delhi, 2008.

(i) Jaiswal, Suvira, *Origin, function and dimensions of change,* New Delhi, Manohar Publishers and distributors, 1998.

Chapter - 8

Socio-Economic Causes of the Ethnic Conflict in Assam

— *Mrs. Reetamoni Kakati*

Introduction

Ethnic conflict is unavoidable and common phenomenon in almost every society. Assam, being a multi-racial, multi-cultural and multi-lingual state, has been hotbed of identity crisis. In Assam, most of the ethnic groups try to maintain their cultural traits, traditions to strengthen their social status as well as economic and political status and this consciousness initiates competition, conflict and crisis among the ethnic groups. The recent socio-economic and political situation in Assam cannot be viewed without placing ethnicity as a major component. Ethnicity in the context of wider multi-cultural society refers to intergroup relations and it originates in inequality. It is a process by which people become more conscious of their group identity which culminates into inter-ethnic conflict leading to social unrest in a multi cultural society. The multi-ethnic and multi-cultural setting of Assam provides a fertile soil for the development of the notion of ethno nationalism and other forms of identity quest. Assam is pulled asunder by ethno national feelings and movements in all parts of the state. In Assam, ethnic conflict and insurgency problem are interwoven in many cases. There are so many cases of ethnic conflict found in Assam. The conflict between the Assamese and

Bengali speaking groups, the anti-foreigners movement in the periods 1979-85, the long-standing Assamese-Nagaland border conflict, the Bodo and the Muslim conflict in 1993, 1996, 2008 and 2012, the Karbi-Kuki conflict in 2003-04 etc are the witnessed various ethnic conflict in Assam. These conflicts have its historical importance in present social setting of Assamese society. This paper is a modest attempt to highlight some socio-economic issues/ causes in terms of existing scenario of ethnic conflict of Assam. Ethnic problems of Assam can be viewed from two different angles-

(1) Caste Hindus versus different ethnic/ tribal groups.
(2) Immigrants (especially Bangladeshi influx) versus Assamese people.

Causes of Ethnic Conflict in Asaam

There are many causes, which are responsible for ethnic crisis or conflict and insurgency in Assam, i.e., deprivation in various socio-economic, geographical spheres, irregular distribution of wealth and development programmes, exploitation, Assamese chauvinism etc. are the basic causes of ethnic conflict. But among these reason, socio-economic dimension is the most outstanding one.

Social Causes of Ethnic Conflict in Assam

1. **Social hatred and seclusion by the Caste Hindus**

   In Assam, caste system plays an important role in socio-economic and political system. Accordingly, there arise some limitations in socio-political mobilization of lower caste people and they suffer from a sense of hatred and are placed seclusively by the caste Hindus. A sense of oppression and deprivation had created a crisis of identity and identity consciousness among different ethnic groups in Assam. For example, generally, high caste/ tribe people do not want to mix up with the low caste in some social situation as they are inferior in social ladder. And high caste/tribe people talk about the abolition of untouchability and caste system but politically they continue this process through the process of 'Neo- Racism'.

2. **Assamese Chauvinism by the Caste Hindus**

   In Assam, Caste Hindus always has been trying to place their establishment in every aspects of social, political and economic life by the notion of Assamese chauvinism. As a result, most of the ethnic groups dissatisfy with them and this led to various ethnic problems and conflicts. In Assam, the caste Hindus always tried to apply the power to establish their social control through administration, education, culture and economic organization. As a result, it would be sure that other ethnic groups began to dissatisfy with Caste Hindus and Government for which they began to arise ethnic crisis and conflict ultimately. In Assamese society, for example, we see; most of the high caste/tribe people feel Assamese chauvinism and they put their seat in *Namghar* in the last line. It is differently treated only for those people, who have high power, education and occupation in the society. This system is prevalent not only in social sphere but also at our home.

3. **Limited Scope of Social Assimilation in the Hindu Social System**

   There are some limitations in the assimilation process in Assam. Every ethnic group along with immigrants faces some problems to assimilate themselves with the mainstream of national life in which a state of conformity arise. All ethnic groups are different from each other in their cultural traits and they are trying to preserve their own culture which consequently hinders the entire process of assimilation. For Example, Assamese society is caste ridden society and thereby processes endogamy. But, in spite of The Special Marriage Act 1954, most of the Assamese people do not like to permit their spouse to get marry with other caste people.

4. **Expansion of Education Among the Tribals**

Education alone is a main weapon which will upgrade the economic and social status of the every ethnic group. Now, the literacy rate among the tribal is increasing day by day. Due to education they are becoming conscious of their rights and privileges. On the other hand, they get much opportunity in social, political and educational spheres as a result of safeguard and reservation system of Indian constitution. So they can raise their social as well as economic status. The new emerging elite of ethnic groups are able to influence the administrative machinery and whenever they feel inequality in distribution, it lead to crisis, which ultimately gives birth of conflict with the government. Literacy rate of Assam is 63.25 percent (according to 2001 census) and 73.18 percent (according to 2011 census). While literacy rate of Schedule Tribe population is 62.5 percent (according to 2001 census) and 73 percent (according to 2011 census). It is shown that literacy rate for both tribal and non tribal peoples increasing from 2001 to 2011. Moreover, there are so many educational schemes for the tribal like **National Overseas Scholarship (NOS) for ST students for studying abroad, Development of Bilingual Primer, Post Matric Scholarship for Schedule Tribe Students, Pre Matric Scholarship for Schedule Tribe Students, Hostel for Schedule Tribe Students girls' and boys'** etc. have been applied for the educational development of the tribal.

Economic Causes of Ethnic Conflict in Assam

1. **Excessive dependence on Agriculture**

   Generally, Assam's tribal economy is agro-based which unfortunately lacks any economic mobility. They do not produce anything for trading purpose but only for consumption. They adopt traditional ways, methods and artifacts in agriculture for which they fail to produce any surplus amount of crops for which their social and economic status remains stagnant. From the very beginning of planning, the Govt. of Assam tries to introduce multi-crop pattern, mechanized system of ploughing, irrigation, sowing and harvesting. Further, there were introduction of several schemes to make the state agriculture market oriented and profitable. In spite of all these, people of Assam unable to take these advantages due to absence of proper knowledge and lack of consciousness for which economy remains underdeveloped.

2. **Tribal Land Alienation**

   The transfer and alienation of tribal lands in both hill and plains to non-tribal is one of the major causes of ethnic conflict and the large-scale transfer of tribal belt and block areas to the hands of Government and landlords, immigrant like Bangladeshis, Nepalis pose serious threat to the tribal habitation. In this respect, the role of politicians and govt. agencies are noticeable. These factors are bound to create serious crisis in tribal population of Assam. For example, Out of 3, 02,545 Bighas of total land of Bijni Tribal Block, an areas covering 66,786 Bighas was de-notified in 1951 and in1952 for constituting Reserve Forest.

3. **Government's Inability to Upgrade the Living Condition of the Tribes**

   The Government of Assam is unable to upgrade the living condition of the tribal people due to the negligence and indifference of the central government, inefficiency of the state government, rampant corruption prevailing top to the bottom of administration. Therefore, Assam remained a village based agricultural state, although it is rich in natural resources. Though there are some constitutional (**Article 330, 332, 334, 338, 342, 275(i), 164, 46** etc) and legislative measures and programmes for the upliftment of the tribes and various development strategies are adopted in the five-year plans especially in Eight plan in which the beneficiary of the Integrated Rural development program are of 50% for the Schedule tribe families the condition of the tribal remains unchanged.

4. Unemployment Among the Educated Youth

Now, unemployment is a devastating problem in Assam. The economic backwardness and lack of job opportunities resulting from inadequate use of natural resources, underdeveloped infrastructure and absence of development not only in the secondary and tertiary sectors but also in agricultural sectors have made the people, especially the educated youth easy prey to the secessionist groups. The tea and oil industries have failed to provide much needed employment opportunities for development of the region. The unemployment problem in fact, is the main reason of ethnic conflict in Assam. A notable scheme named **Vocational Training in Tribal Areas** for all the state, union territories and other Associations of central government try to develop the skill of the ST youth for a variety of jobs as well as self employment and to improve their socio-economic condition by enhancing their income. According to 2001 Census, 43.2 percent of the STs have been registered as workers, which is below the aggregated national figure for STs (49.1 percent). Of the total workers 65.3 percent are main workers and 34.7 percent marginal workers. WPR of 35.8 percent among females is high though lower than males (50.5 percent). Gender wise disparity is, however, distinct in case of main workers; 80.9 percent among males and only 42.6 percent among females are main workers.

5. **Poverty**

   Assam suffers from poverty due to insufficient land for agriculture, lack of proper education, absence of knowledge and inability of state and central governments, corruption etc. Flood problem is another factor of poverty of Assam. The recurring flood of Assam badly affects the people of Lakhimpur, Dhemaji, Sonitpur, Jorhat and many other districts for which they have to pay a lot. Consequently, their economic condition is degrading day by day. There are so many schemes allocated by central and state government for the welfare of the tribal and non tribal people. Two worthwhile schemes of Government for tribal people are **Special Central Assistance to Tribal Sub-Scheme (SCA to TSS)** and **Scheme of Grant-in-Aid to voluntary organization working for the Welfare of the STs (1953-54)** for poverty eradication in tribal areas.

Conclusion

In conclusion, it becomes clear that some social and economic aspects act as major factors of uprising ethnic conflict in Assam. So, in order to grab privileges and opportunities in social, political and economic sphere, the ethnic groups struggle among themselves which lead to a serious social and political tension in Assam. Due to gradual destruction of forest, tribal people deprived of a supplementary source of both food and income. As a result, economic degradation arises in their day today life. We can say that now it becomes urgent to establish a balance among different ethnic, indigenous and aboriginal folks.

Instead of over-looking the burning problems of ethnic conflicts, we should try to find out some amicable solutions for those problems and this goal can be attained only with the dedicated involvement of all public and government. If we can maintain a good sense of understanding among different ethnic groups, promote education for the much needed proper development of the various ethnic groups, central and state government pay some special attention and provide more fund for the overall development of entire region and utmost care should be taken to ensure the fruitful utilization of the money we will be able to solve some of the conflict in Assam. In this regard, the leading social organization or association like Asom Sahitya Sabha, Mising Kebang, AASU, Satra Sangha, Yuva Satra Parisad etc. should promote peace and social harmony among different ethnic groups in Assam. They should fight against different secessionist forces. Ethnic conflict has its immense effect on national integration and nation building in any society. Therefore, we may deduce the parameters of the ethnic conflict in support of the respective society by adopting collective effort through various means. As a citizen of India in general, Assam in particular we should carry out such studied to find out the causes of the problems and try to take amicable solution.

References

1. Borpujari H.K. (1998): *North-East India-problems, Policies & Prospects,* Delhi, Spectrum Publications.
2. Bordoloi B.N. (ed): *Transfer and Alianation of Tribal Land in Assam,* Assam, Guwahati, Tribal Research Institute.
3. Danda Ajit K. et.al, (2006): *Social Unrest.* Kolkata, Indian National Confederation and Academy of Anthropologists.
4. Hazarika Mantu & Chutia Thagendra (ed) (2014): *Ethnic Groups in North East India*, Guwahati, Kasturi Printers & Publishers.
5. Padhi Soubhagya Ranjan & Padhi Biswjita (ed) (2010): *Tribal Development in India*, Delhi, Manglam Publications.
6. Patiri Pranjal & Dutta Dr. Anupam (2017): Assam College Teachers' Association JOURNAL, Guwahati, Frquency of Publication.

7. Shankar Rao C.N. (2016): Sociology of Indian Society, New Delhi, S, Chand & Company Pvt. Ltd.
8. Singh, B.P. (1999): *The problem of Change.* Translated by Akhil R. Dutta, New Delhi, National Book Trust.
9. http://pib.gov.in, Retrieved on September, 2019.
10. https://m.jagranjosh.com, Retrieved on September, 2019.
11. https://www.culturalsurvival.org, Retrieved on September, 2019.
12. https://www.firstpost.com, Retrieved on October, 2019.
13. https://unemployment, Retrieved on October, 2019.
14. https://tribal.nic.in/writ
15. https://www.india.gov.in
16. Censusinindia.gov.in

Chapter - 9

India's North-east a Historical & Geographical Perspective Covering the Study Area of the Dhansiri (South) River Basin

— *Dr. Shashwati Nath*

History of the North-East India

A fraction of North East India is described as *Kamrupa* in Indian history. Ancient *Kamrupa* had four divisions as *Kam-peeth, Ratna-peeth, Swarna-peeth* and *Soumar-peeth.* Later on the area was a part of *Soumar-peeth.* The area between the Bhairabi (Bharali) river in the west to the Dikrai River close to present Sadiya in the east was known as *Soumar-peeth.* (Gohainbaruah, 1937). It covered the present Lakhimpur, Dhemaji, Tinsukia, Dibrugarh, Sibsagar, Jorhat, Golaghat and part of Sonitpur districts. Until the first quarter of the thirteenth century AD, the *Soumar-peeth* was ruled by the *Barahi, Matak* and *Moran* rulers (Gohainbaruah, 1937 pp. 56-57). Sukapha belonged to the Shan or Tai ethnic group of the Irrawaddy valley of Myanmar. He occupied *Soumar-peeth* and overcome the *Barahi, Matak* and *Moran* rulers. Myth says that Sukapha was the grandchild of Lord Indra, the king of heaven. It is, therefore, the word *Swargadeo* (meaning king) is preset to the name of each of the kings of that dynasty (Gohainbaruah, 1937 p 50). The kingdom of *Swargadeo* Sukapha was afterward named as 'Asom' which means uneven. *Swargadeo* Sukapha ruled his new kingdom with unprecedented spirit and power. Before him, no ruler in Soumar-peeth could show such valor (Gohainbaruah, 1937 p. 57). During the British rule, the word Asom was spelt as Assam. There are, however, little other misinformation as well regarding the origin of the word 'Assam'. During his reign, *Swargadeo* Sukapha moved his capital from place to place and finally located at Charaideo, Gargaon and Jorhat.

Swargadeo Shivasingha was ruled in 1636 AD. Under conditions, he selected Ambika, one of his queens, as the 'Bor-raja (the care taker queen). She ruled the Ahom kingdom from 1642 to 1663 AD. During her term a large tank was dug as 'Shivasagar'. The Shiva-dol, which is whispered to be the tallest Shiva temple in Asia, was stiffed at one of the banks of the Shivasagar tank (Barbaruah 1981, pp. 242-246). In course of time, the area around the tank was known as Shivasagar. During British phase the word 'Shivasagar' started to be spelt as 'Sibsagar'. Assam came in the British rule following the Yandabu Treaty in 1826. A decade later on, in 1836, the British rulers composed two districts as 'Sibsagar' and 'Lakshimpur' (Allen, 1906). Sibsagar persisted to be a district of Assam since afterward. During that time these two districts were much larger than their present size.

The three districts forming the present study area were amalgamated as a single district and were known as Sibsagar. The present three districts were its three sub-divisions. The Sibsagar district of 1971 (which is the base year for the present study) has been divided into three different districts as Golaghat, Jorhat and Sibsagar. These divisions were made in the year 1983.

Location and Extension

The extreme north eastern corner of India has a bunch of seven states bordered by foreign countries like Bhutan, China, Myanmar and Bangladesh. This group of seven states is linked to the mainland of India through a narrow piece of land consists of Arunachal Pradesh, Nagaland, Manipur, Mizoram, Tripura, Meghalaya and Assam. Assam has the central place among these seven states. Assam only is surrounded by seven other states of India and two countries Bhutan and Bangladesh.

Assam has Bhutan and Arunachal Pradesh along its entire northern boundary. The state of Arunachal Pradesh is also bordering Assam on the east. Nagaland, Manipur, Mizoram. Tripura and Meghalaya are the states located to the south of Assam. Bangladesh is also sharing a small portion of the southern boundary of Assam. Along with West Bengal, Bangladesh again shares the western boundary of Assam.

The mighty river Brahmaputra flows through the state from east to west dividing the state into two unequal halves being the north bank and the south bank. Assam has its major part of the geographical area within the Brahmaputra valley. Excepting a small gap in the west, the Brahmaputra valley is surrounded from all sides by hills and mountains. These hills and mountains include the foothills of Himalayas on the north, the hills and mountains of the Naga-Patkai range on the east as well as south-east, the Barail range and the table land of Meghalaya on the south. As the Brahmaputra valley is surrounded by hills and mountains, the rain water rushes to the valley through numerous rivers and streams coming out of these hills soon after a downpour. Under the impact of monsoon, which causes rainfall during summer, the river Brahmaputra and many of its tributaries cause flood during the summer months from May to October every year.

The study area comprises three districts of Assam on the southern bank of Brahmaputra (Fig.1). These three districts, form west to east are Golaghat, Jorhat and Sibsagar. Majuli, which is often called as the world's largest river island is a sub-division of the Jorhat district and is located along the northern margins of the study area. In fact, the study area lies between the hills of Nagaland on the south and the river Brahmaputra on the north. The districts of Dibrugarh and Karbi Anglong are bordering the study area on the east and west respectively.

Geographically, the study area lies little north of tropic of cancer and to the south of the eastern Himalayan ranges. The study area is stretching from 25°482323 north to 27°162303 north parallels. Longitudinally, the area lies between 93°172153 east and 95°222393 east meridians. The total area covered by the three districts is 8731.77 sq km. It includes 3358.80 sq km under Golaghat district, 2730.47 sq km under Jorhat district and 2642.50 sq km under Sibsagar district. As such, the study area covers 11.13 percent of the total geographical area of Assam. The Brahmaputra and its tributaries cover 72 percent of the total geographical area of Assam (Bora, 2001, p. 19). Based on this, the present study area covers 15.50 percent of the Brahmaputra valley within the state of Assam.

Assam and Nagaland have a common boundary of 347 km between the two states. Nagaland, basically has a hilly topography while Assam is a state with its major part in the plains. As many as five districts of Assam, namely North Cachar hills, Karbi Anglong, Golaghat, Jorhat and Sibsagar are located along this boundary. Of these five districts, North Cachar Hills and Karbi Anglong have hilly topography and the remaining Golaghat, Jorhat and Sibsagar districts extent over the Brahmaputra plain. A distinct zone of foothills exists in these three districts along the Assam-Nagaland boundary. These foothills belong to the Naga-Patkai range. In fact, it is a geographical boundary separating two very important physiographic divisions of the north eastern part of the country.

The Brahmaputra valley has an east-west orientation and it exhibits four distinct physiographic units such as (i) the northern foothills, (ii) the north and south bank plains, (iii) the floodplain and char-lands and (iv)the southern foothills (Bora, Pp.76, 2001).

River Brahmaputra borders the study area on the north. Throughout the whole of its course through the present study area, the Brahmaputra is bounded on the south by a belt of flooded land wider near the Dhansiri mouth.

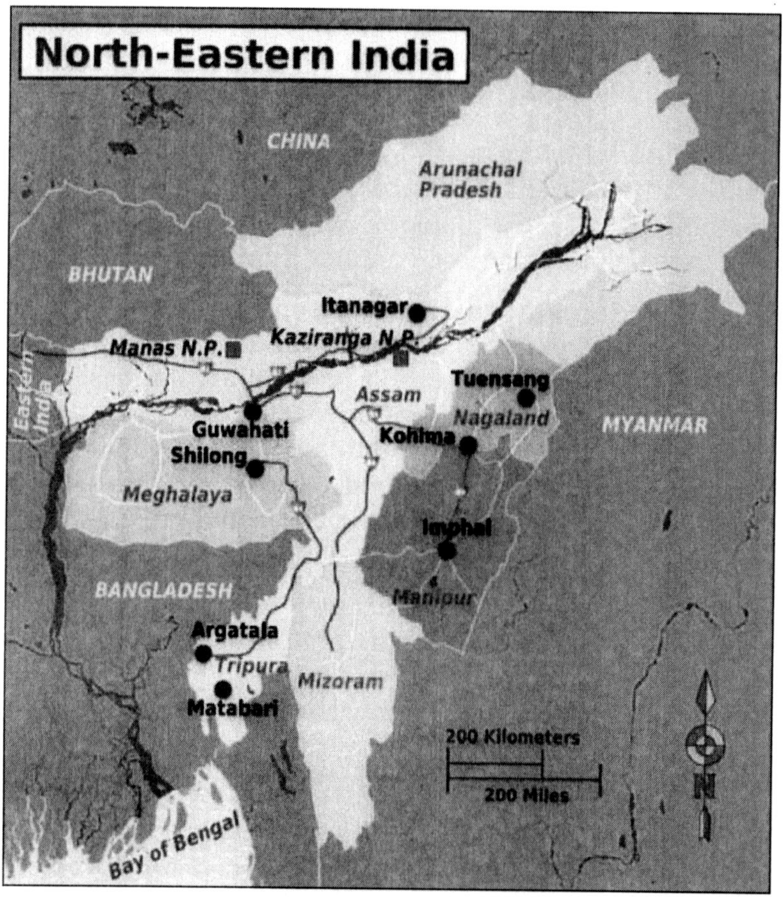

Fig. 1: Map of the study area.

In between the river Brahmaputra and the foothills there exists an extensive plain composed of new and old alluvium. This plain is the largest physiographic unit of the study area and it covers 64.12 percent of the geographical area of the study area. As it exists between the foothills and the river Brahmaputra, a gentle slope exists from south to north and a large number of streams and rivers like Dhansiri, Bhogdoi, Janji, Dikhow and Disang come down from the foothills following the slope. In fact, this plain is formed under the erosional and gradational activities of the rivers and streams.

Drainage

Brahmaputra and its numerous large and small tributaries, Assam is really a land of rivers. The hills and mountains, which surround the Brahmaputra valley from nearly all sides, give it a unique geographical location enabling it to receive copious rainfall under the south-west monsoon during the summer months.

The Brahmaputra forms a complex river system characterized by the most dynamic and unique water and sediment transport pattern. It is the fourth largest river in the world in terms of average water discharge at the mouth with a flow of 19830m**3**s-**1** or cubic meter per second. Again, it is the second river only to the Yellow river of China in amount of sediment transported per unit of drainage area (Goswami, 1985, 1988).

As the Brahmaputra is bordered by the hills of Nagaland to the south, several large and small rivers and streams come down from these hills while, few of them including Dhansiri and Dikhow have their source beyond the foothills and they flow across the mountainous topography of the state of Nagaland.

Dhansiri, one of the major south bank tributaries of Brahmaputra comes across the hills of Nagaland following a fault line. The upper course of the river passes through a thick forest cover in the hills of Nagaland and several reserved forests of Assam. In its course through the plains the river is extremely meandering in nature and has formed a large number of cut-off lakes on both sides of its

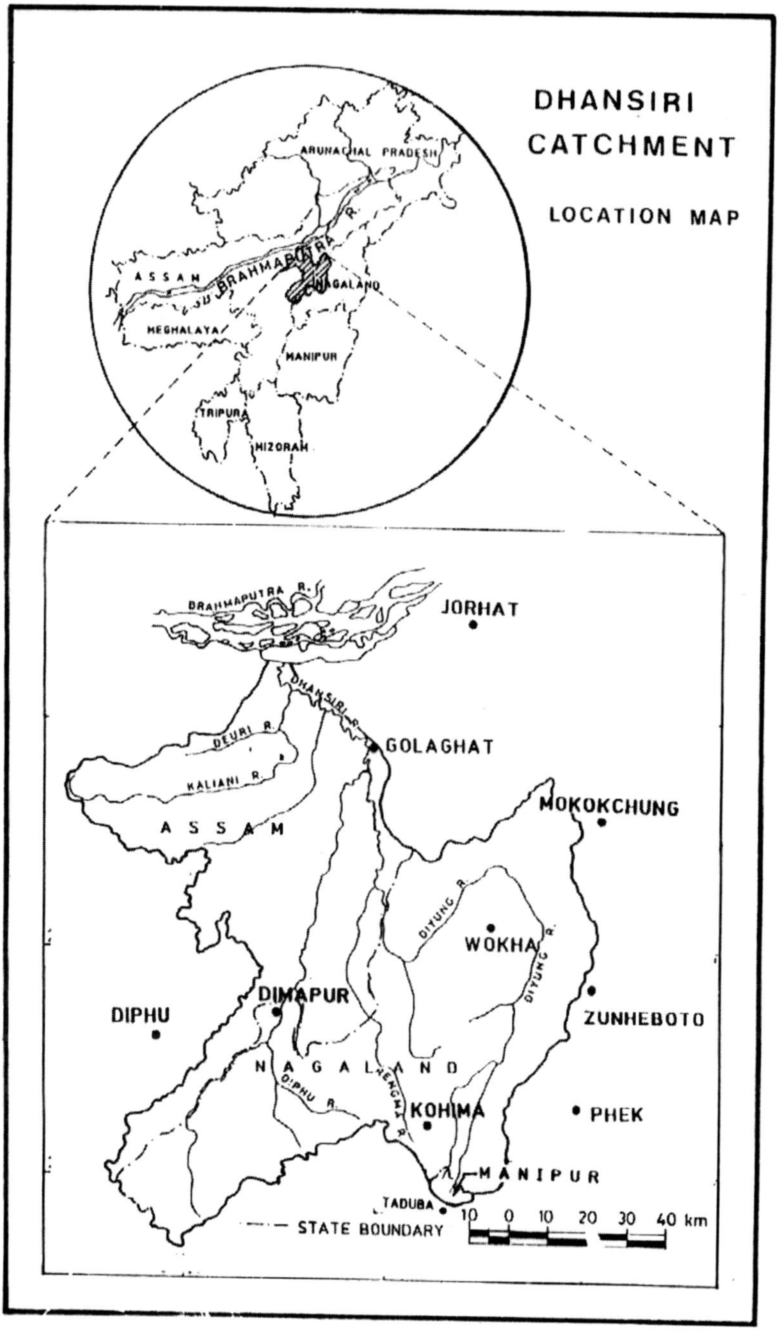

Location Map

channel (ARSAC Report, 1990). Dhansiri is perhaps one of the most meandering rivers of the world. It has a channel length of 352 km from source to mouth. Inside the geographical territory of Assam the river has several tributaries of its own. The Doyang is the largest tributary of Dhansiri. In fact, Doyang is nearly two times larger than Dhansiri and in that context Dhansiri should be treated to be the tributary of Doyang (Sharma, 2008). The other tributaries of Dhansiri are Diphu, Chunga-jan, Deopani, Nambar, Doigrung and Kaliani. Among these Deopani, Nambar, Doigrung and Kaliani have their source in the hills of Karbi Anglong and the others have their source in the hills of Nagaland. Each of these rivers has their own sub-tributaries and all these have together formed a complex drainage network covering 12584 sq km area of the basin of river Dhansiri (Sharma, 2008). Before meeting the master stream, Dhansiri meets Gelabil at a place called Kuruabahi Rangagora of Golaghat district. In fact, Gelabil is an abandoned channel of Brahmaputra (Gazetteer, 1906, p. 8) which now carries the joint discharge of Bhogdoi and Kakadonga to Dhansiri. As per historical documents Bhogdoi was known as Disoi and was a tributary of Brahmaputra. During the last two centuries Disoi (or Bhogdoi) has undergone tremendous changes of its course due to physical and anthropogenic factors. The river network of the study area is shown in Fig. 2.

Soils

As the major part of the study area is in the flood plain, the soils are mostly alluvial. The northern areas, which are nearer to the river Brahmaputra have new alluvium, while the southern areas or areas near the foothills have old alluvium. The areas with older alluvium are the best sites for the cultivation of tea. Accordingly, the areas with older alluvium are dotted with a large number of tea gardens. The entire area is under humid sub-tropical climate and it receives well distributed rainfall from May to October.

Land Use

Land use is associated with putting up of parcel of land into its productive purposes. It is a dynamic concept because, the characteristics of heterogeneity and fertility differentials or the possibility of the use for production of alternative outputs of a plot of land make people to choose their land to be put under uses in such a way that they could maximize the output (Das, 1976). In fact, the land use in an area is the cumulative outcome of the historical events, the interaction of the economic forces with the natural environment, and the value of the society (Singh and Dhillon, 1989, p. 326).

Areas under different land use in the study area :

Sl. No.	*Landuse*	*Area in Sq.km*	*Percentage*
1.	Agriculture	6,816.27	57.06
2.	Forest	4,677.36	39.15
3.	Tea Garden	250.22	2.09
4.	Fallow grazing land	80.05	0.67
5.	Miscellaneous	123.10	1.03

Source: Calculated by the researcher on the data collected from Government officials.

The land utilization demonstrates variation in four facets. The first is the expansion of the urban areas. The second reason is the conversion of the land under miscellaneous crops and paddy fields into tea gardens. This leads to a slow and steady increase in the land under plantation crops. The reserved forests of the foothills are dotted with many small tea gardens all along the Assam-Nagaland border.

The third is the clearing and felling of forests in the foothills and the piedmont areas for the purpose of settlement and cultivation (including the practice of shifting cultivation). These are happening within the Notified Forest Areas. Consequently, the area under degraded forest and cropland (including plantation) is increasing with time.

Sibsagar, which encompassed the entire study area in the past, has been a centre of Assamese culture since long back. It was the administrative head quarter of the *Ahom* rulers. The extensive and fertile plains coupled with the cultural heritage of the area support a large population base.

Population

As per 2001 census, the total population of the study area was 2997236 persons (11.24 percent of the total population of the state) of which 1552777 (or 51.81 percent) were males and 1444459 (or 48.19 percent) were females. The sex ratio of the study area is 930 and it is lower than the state average (935 females against every thousand males). The area has only 11.66 percent urban population and remaining 88.33 percent people live in the rural areas. The religious composition of the population of the study area shows that 89.04 percent of the people are Hindus. The Muslims, Christians, Buddhists, Sihkhs and Jains constitute respectively 6.95, 3.31, 0.32, 0.14 and 0.05 percent of the total population of the area. The castes among the Hindus of the study area include the Ahom, Chutiya, Kalita, Koch, Kaivarta, Brahmins, Keot, Yogi, Sut, Kayastha, Kachari, Mishing, Mikir (Karbi) and the tea garden workers (Taher, 2000).

Source: Statistical Hand Book , Assam (2008)

Transport, Communication and Development Activities

The study area enjoys all modes of transportation and it is well connected to the rest of the India. Three National highways (NH) pass through the area. The NH-37 passes across the study area. Again, NH-39 and NH-61 originate from NH-37 and they connect Nagaland with Assam. The *Dhodar ali* (*ali* means road) is a notable road. The *Gar ali, Cheuni ali, Bor ali, Kamarbandha ali, Rohdoi ali* are some other examples of this kind. These roads are now maintained by the state Public Works Department (PWD).

The railway line between Guwahati and Tinsukia runs across all the districts of the study area. This single-line railway tract has a loop line which originates from the Furkating Junction and moving via Golaghat, Numaligarh, Baruabamun gaon and Jorhat Town, it ends at the same railway tract at Mariani Junction. Another branch line has recently been opened from Simaluguri Junction to Dibrugarh via Moran.

During the British rule in Assam, the river Brahmaputra was used as a water way and steamer services were introduced for transportation of goods mainly tea and passengers. In addition to these steamer services, country boats were widely used in Brahmaputra and its tributaries for both passenger and goods. In absence of bridges across the rivers, the country boats provided ferry services at a number of points, locally known as *ghats.*

The religious composition of the population of the study area shows that 89.04 percent of the people are Hindus. The Muslims, Christians, Buddhists, Sihkhs and Jains constitute respectively 6.95, 3.31, 0.32, 0.14 and 0.05 percent of the total population of the area. The castes among the Hindus of the study area include the Ahom, Chutiya, Kalita, Koch, Kaivarta, Brahmins, Keot, Yogi, Sut, Kayastha, Kachari, Mishing, Mikir (Karbi) and the tea garden workers (Taher, 2000).

Conclusion

River basin represents distinctive pattern of interaction and inter-relations between men and environment. Rivers are recognized as the lifeline of the people and the society. Geologically, historically, culturally and economically, rivers have massive importance to the riverbank population.

Men and rivers both are products of nature. The great human interest in settling down in the bankline of rivers is due to umber of positive environmental factors. A review of historical literature reveals that the Tigris, the Euphrates, the Nile, the Indus and the Yangtze are the cradles of great human civilizations. The Brahmaputra river is assumed as a great multiplicity of culture, ethnic, social, economy linguistic groups accompanied with panoramic environment occupy an unique habitats of the basin. The Brahmaputra and its tributary Dhansiri (South) is no exception.The settlement of population in the river side is determined by the old trend of settlement except in urban centers. Physiography and environment both not only determine the site selection but also affect rural urban dichotomy of the area. Most of the site selection for the age old rural settlement is directly based on relief (slope) considerations. Different aspects of the geomorphologic (geographical shape, size etc.) consideration taken in to account for settlement is the land stability and availability of natural sources of water, particularly, springs for drinking purposes.

Thus, in view of the present situation, it can be stated that the Dhansiri (south) river valley shows a conspicuous environmental landscape and mixed multi-structural scenario of cultural frameworks among all people where they try to adjust themselves suitably and stay together.

References

1. Annual Mayhem in Assam in 'Floods, flood plains and Environmental Myths' Centre for Sci. and Env. Pub.3, New Delhi (1985), pp. 71 – 94.
2. Barman, R., 1986: Geomorphology of Kamrup District – A Morphometric and Quantitative Analysis, pp. 245.
3. Bhagabati, A.K, Bora, A.K., and Kar, B.K. (2001) : Geography of Assam, Rajesh Publications, New Delhi, pp. 36, 39, 40, 42.
4. Borthakur, M. (1986) : Weather and Climate of North East India, North Eastern Geographer, Vol. 18, No. 1 and 2.
5. Barman, R.N. and Das, R., (2008): Agriculture in Riverine Situation: Analysis of Technology Adoption and Constraints of Development of Char Areas of North Bank Plains Zone in Assam, New Delhi, pp. 304 – 305.

6. Coleman, J.M., (1969) : Brahmaputra River : Channel Processes and Sedimentation, Sedimentary Geology, Vol. 3, No. 2/3, pp. 129-139, 166 – 180.
7. Das, M.M., (1981) : Pattern of Soil Distribution in Assam, North Eastern Geographer, Vol. XIII, No. 1 and 2.
8. Das, M.M., and Das, H., 1989 : Land Use Pattern in the Pagladia – Puthimari Basin, Assam, N-Eastern Geographer, Vol. 21, No. 1 and 2, pp. 9 – 24.
9. Dasgupta, A.B., and Biswas, A.K., (2000) : Geology of Assam, Geological Society of India, Bangalore, p. 13.
10. Goswami, D.C., (1997) : Brahmaputra River Basin Forestry. In Forestry and Key Asian Watershed, Myint AK, Hofer T (Eds), ICIMOD : Kathmandu; pp. 32 – 37.
11. Sarma, R., and Bora, A.K. (1995) : Impact of Slope on Land Use in the Dhaleswari Basin of N E India, Hill Geographer Vol. 11, No. 1 and 2, pp. 13 – 19.
12. Sarma, R. and Goswami, D.C., (2001) : Fluvial Geomorphology and Basin Ecology of the Jia Dhansiri (North) River Basin, Assam, Indian Journal of Geomorphology, Vol.6, No.1 and 2, pp. 91 – 106.

Chapter - 10

Problem Faced by Secondary School Students in Sonitpur and Lakhimpur Districts of Assam

— Dr. Dipti Saikia

Introduction

Education is the most powerful instrument for overall development and all round achievement of the nations. Education is a process which aims at the complete development of human's personality and prepares them for the battle of life so as to enable them shoulder their responsibility towards the progress of the society. It is a process to develop the intellectual faculties of the man. It makes man civilized, refined and cultured. For civilized and socialized society education is only means. It is a systematic process through which a child or a man acquires knowledge, experience, skill and sound attitude. Education is the process, by which society deliberately transmits its accumulated knowledge, skills and values from one generation to another. It can be seen as wings for the progress of the human beings.

Secondary education is one of the important stages of formal pattern of education. Secondary education is a stage of education that is imparted after Elementary education and before higher education. In today's world secondary education has a vital mission of creating a bright future for individuals and nations alike. Secondary education is a crucial stage in the educational hierarchy as it prepares the students for higher education and also for the world of work. Classes IX and X constitute the secondary stage, whereas classes XI and XII are designated as the higher secondary stage. The rigor of the secondary and higher secondary stage, enables Indian students to complete successfully for education and for jobs globally. Therefore, it is absolutely essential to strengthen this stage by providing greater access and also by improving quality in a significant way. It has to play a vital role in the educational system of the community. But the main defect of secondary education is its aimlessness. Secondary education must have definite aims related to practical life. The study specially designed to identify the problems that affect secondary school students in Sonitpur and Lakhimpur districts of Assam.

Objective of the Study

- To identify the problems faced by Students at Secondary school level in Sonitpur and Lakhimpur districts of Assam.

Methodology

The present study based on descriptive survey method of research. It is based on mainly data collection through a sample survey conducted in the Sonitpur and Lakhimpur districts, the researcher selected a sample of 10 secondary schools from two selected districts (10 schools from each district) by adopting random sampling technique.

Discussion

In order to identify the problems faced by secondary school students the researcher developed a questionnaire and administrated on a sample of 200 students from two selected districts (100 students from each district). The researcher visited various schools to administer questionnaires on the targeted sample. The questionnaire contains 25 items and the detail analysis is given district wise:

Table: Showing percentage responses made by the secondary school students in Sonitpur and Lakhimpur districts of Assam

Sl. No.	Items	Options	Sonitpur		Lakhimpur	
			Yes %	No %	Yes %	No %
1.	Distance from the house to school	i. Below 1 km.	26	74	14	86
		ii. Between 1-5 km.	74	26	85	15
		iii. Above 5 km.	-	100	01	99
2.	Notebooks and supplementary Guide books in time If no, reasons-	-	60	40	56	44
		i. Poor financial condition of the parents	30	10	20	24
		ii. Lack of awareness of the parents	15	25	21	23
		iii. Do not ask for materials from the parents	10	30	08	32
3.	Sufficient study hours at home if no, reasons-	-	75	25	80	20
		i. Involved in domestic work	15	10	09	11
		ii. Income generating activities.	10	15	11	09
4.	Parents encourage you to go to school and study	-	80	20	100	-
5.	Parents give equal opportunity to sons and daughter	-	75	25	80	20
6.	Sufficient sitting arrangements in your school	-	68	32	76	24
7.	Understand the lesson taught by teacher If no, reasons-	-	70	30	77	23
		i. Could not understand what is taught in the class	15	15	12	11
		ii. Medium of instruction	10	20	11	12
8.	Reading materials available in your school	i. Text and Reference book	100	-	100	-
		ii. Encyclopedia	-	100	-	100
		iii. Journals, magazines & newspaper	56	44	60	40
		iv. Dictionary.	50	50	68	32

(Contd...)

9.	use of teaching aids in the classroom	-	100	-	100	-
		Please tick mark on the following items- i. Globe	73	27	60	30
		ii. Maps	100	-	90	10
		iii. Educational charts	20	80	50	40
		iv. Chalk, duster, pointer.	100	-	100	-
10.	Free textbooks from your school	-	100	-	100	-
11.	Most difficult subject-	i. English	45	55	60	40
		ii. Science	25	75	20	80
		iii. Mathematics	50	50	68	32
		iv. Social studies	65	35	70	30
12.	Happy in attending the school If no, reasons-	-	100	-	98	02
		i. School building is not attractive.	-	100	-	100
		ii. Classrooms are too small	-	100	02	98
		iii. Lessons are not understandable	-	100	-	100
		iv. Disliking of the teachers.	-	100	-	100
13.	Find your curriculum-	i. Easy	-	100	-	100
		ii. Tough	33	67	26	74
		iii. Medium.	67	33	74	26
14.	Recreational facilities available in the school If yes-	-	81	19	50	50
		i, Musical instrument	36	45	50	50
		ii. Sports goods	45	36	40	60
		iii. other facility	-	100	-	100
15.	Separate toilet facilities in the school If yes-	-	100	-	100	-
		i. Sanitary	55	45	60	40
		ii. Semi-pucca toilet	60	40	40	60
		iii. Kacha toilet	10	90	-	100
16.	Drinking water in the school If yes-	-	100	-	100	-
		i. Well	10	90	10	90
		ii. Water pump	12	88	06	94
		iii. Hand pump	13	87	15	85
		iv. Pipeline	67	33	70	30
17.	Playground and play materials in the school	-	100	-	100	-
18.	Leisure time activities	i. Drawing	12	88	-	100
		ii. Playing	84	16	60	40
		iii. Music and culture	20	80	-	100
		iv. None of these	0	0	40	60
19.	Friendly and encouraging teachers	-	72	28	60	40
20.	Arrangement for special coaching class	-	20	80	10	90
21.	Teachers are regular and sincere in teaching	-	73	27	90	10

(Contd...)

22.	Conduct class tests regularly	-	83	17	89	12
23.	Take part in co-curricular activities	-	55	45	70	30
24.	Principal visit the class	i. Regularly	-	100	07	93
		ii. Rarely	72	28	33	67
		iii. Occasionally	27	73	60	40
25.	School inspector visit the school	-	75	25	80	20

- **Problems faced by the Secondary School Students in Sonitpur District of Assam**

The above table shows, the responses made by students regarding problems faced at secondary school level in Sonitpur district of Assam. The first item is relating to distance of school, only 26% students indicated that distance from school to home is below 1 km. and 74% students stated 1-5 km. 40% students reveals that they do not get study materials in time, reasons are: 30% responded poor financial conditions of the parents, 15% lack of awareness among parents and 10% students responded that they do not ask materials from the parents. 25% students do not get sufficient study hours at home because 15% students are involved in domestic work and 10% students are involved in income generating activities. 20% Parents do not encourage their children to go to school and study. 25% students reveal that parents do not give equal opportunity to sons and daughter. 32% students stated that they do not have sufficient sitting arrangements in their school. 30% students stated that they do not understand the lesson taught by the teacher as, 15% could not understand the teaching and 10% because of medium of instruction. 56% students stated that they do have magazines and journals in the schools, only 50% students' reveals that dictionaries are available in their school. 100% students reveals that their teachers used teaching aids in the classrooms but it is very traditional like map, globe charts etc. 45% students are having problem in learning in English, at the same time 25% in Science, 50% in mathematics and 65% in social science. Only 05% students do not feel happy in attending the school regularly. 100% students stated that curriculum is not easy, reasons are: 33% students' finds it tough and 67% finds it medium. Only 19% students stated that recreational facilities are not available in the school. 100% students stated that they have separate toilet facilities in their school, i.e. 55% toilets are sanitary, 60% are semi-pucca and 10% are kacha toilet. 100% students have indicated availability of drinking water facility. 28% students stated that their teachers are not encouraging. 80% students indicated that there is no arrangement for special coaching class for the students. 27% students stated teachers are not regular and sincere in teaching, in case of class test, it was found that 17% teachers do not conduct class test. 45% students reveal that they take part in co-curricular activities. 72% students have indicated that principal rarely visit their classroom and 27% indicated occasionally, 25% students stated that school inspector does not visit their school.

- **Problems faced by the Secondary School Students in Lakhimpur District of Assam**

  Regarding the problems faced by secondary school students of Lakhimpur district of Assam, the first item is about distance of school, 14% students indicated that their distance from school to home is 1 km., 85% student stated 1-5 km. and only 01% students is found above 5 km. 44% of the students reveals that they do not get study materials in time, reasons are: 20% students reveals poor financial conditions of the parents, 21% lack of awareness among parents and 08% do not ask for books from the parents. 20% students do not get sufficient study hours at home because 09% students are involved in domestic work and 11% students involved in income generating activities. 20% student reveals that parents do not give equal opportunity to sons and daughter. 24% students stated that they do not have sufficient sitting arrangements in their school. 23% students stated that they do not understand the lesson taught by the teacher as 12% could not understand the teaching and 11% because of medium of instruction. 60% students stated that they do have magazines and journals in the schools. Only 68% students reveal that dictionaries are available in their school. 100% students reveals that their teachers used teaching aids in the classrooms but it is very traditional like map, globe charts etc. 60% students are having problem in learning in English, at the same time 20% in Science, 68% in mathematics and 70% in social science. Only 02% students do not feel happy in attending the school regularly. 100% students stated that curriculum is not easy, reasons are: 26% students' finds it tough and 74% finds it medium. 50% students stated that recreational facilities are not available in the school. 100% students stated that they have separate toilet facilities in their school, i.e. 60% toilets are sanitary and 40% are semi-pucca toilet. 100% students have indicated availability of drinking water facility, i. e. 10% have well, 15% hand pump, 06% water pump and 70% are pipeline. 60% students responded that they play in the leisure time. 60% students responded that their teachers are friendly and encouraging. 90% students indicated there is no arrangement for special coaching class for students. 10% students stated that teachers are not regular and sincere in teaching. In case of class test, it was found that 12% teachers do not conduct class test. 30% students responded that they do not take part in co-curricular activities. 07% students stated that principal/headmaster regularly visits in the class, 33% students have indicated principal visit their class rarely and 60% indicated occasionally. 20% students stated that school inspector does not visit their school.

Findings and Conclusion

Regarding the problems of secondary school students, it was revealed that most of the students are facing some common problems like – overcrowded classrooms, lack of supplementary materials, setting arrangement, teaching aids, separate toilet facilities, understanding subjects, recreational facilities, medium of instruction, class test, examination system, neglects co-curricular activities, many school suffer from the inadequate number of able and trained teachers, etc.

Therefore, different committee and commissions before and after independence have mentioned various aims of secondary education, but it is not complete by itself. The main defect of secondary education is its aimlessness. For improvement of the secondary education must have definite aim related to practical life. The current secondary education has aggravated the unemployment problem. Therefore, we have to make our secondary education so useful and they become economically independent by having acquired some vocational skills of productive nature. Most of the secondary schools are over-crowded, ill-staffed and suffer from inadequate numbers of teachers and accommodation, infrastructure, teacher training facilities, trained teachers etc. So, to improve the quality of secondary education in Assam immediate attention needs to be provided and also government should provide financial help for improvement of the said problems.

References

Fonseca, J (1996), *Secondary School Education in Twenty – First Century,* the Progress of Education, Vol. LXXI, No. 5.

Hazarika, Mousumee (1996-97), *Problem faced by the Students of the Secondary Schools of the Jagiroad Revenue Town in Learning English,* M. Ed dissertation, Guwahati University Gupta, S.(2008), *Education in Emerging India,* Shipra Publication, Delhi.

Kochhar, S.K. (2009), *Pivotal Issues in Indian Education,* Sterling Publishing House Pvt. Ltd. pp. 14, 15, 118-120.

Anga, Nyokir (2012), *Status of Secondary School Education in Arunachal Pradesh: A Critical Study,* Ph.D. thesis, Rajiv Gandhi University, Arunachal Pradesh, pp. 28 to 60.

www.careerizma.com

https:// www.researchgate.net

www.yourarticlelibrary.com

Chapter - 11

Women Empowerment in North-eastern Region

— Noyanmoni Saikia

Introduction

North-East India is the eastern most region of India representing both a geographical and political administrative division of the country. It comprises eight states - Arunachal Pradesh, Assam, Manipur, Meghalaya, Mizoram, Nagaland, Sikkim and Tripura. The states of eastern region are considered as the backward area in terms of the per capita income. There is lack of development. The geographical area is 262,230 sq. kms. And the population is around 38,857,769. The socioeconomic set up of the state has not been favourable to overall progress. Since it is a multiethnic state with heterogeneous cultural backgrounds, it has been, experiencing insurgency and ethnic conflict for the last three decades because of which not only its economy but also the social structure is wider threat. The worst sufferers in the process are the women. The region is developing on the certain parameters, but to understand the real development we need to focus on the empowerment of women. According to Pandit Jawaharlal Nehru, "If you want to awaken country first awake women. If a women is awakened a family is awakened and if a family is awakened, a village is awakened thereby entire country is awakened" Women's development is directly related to nations development and also one of the most powerful strategies of women empowerment. We cannot deny the fact that women are contributing a lot for overall development of our country. But the truth is that in the modem India the women have always been treated as second class citizen continued to a target the sources of all the violence and ill will towards women. Generally women as well as girls are less likely to access school, to remain in school or to achieve in education, Education helps men and women to claim their rights and to realize their potential in the economic, political and social sphere.

Objectives

The main objectives of the present study are as follows;-

(1) To identify the socio-cultural and economic factors influencing women's empowerment.

(2) To know about the importance of education towards women empowerment.

Methodology

The present study is mainly based on descriptive method and uses secondary data. The data are collected from different Books, Journals, Internet sources, Newspaper etc.

Discussion

The dictionary meaning of the word 'empower' is to give somebody the power or authority to do something or to give somebody more control over their life or the situation they are in. "Power" is the key term in word empowerment. Rowlands suggest four forms of power i.e. power within, power to, power with and power over,. Whereas power within refers to self-esteem and awareness power to refers to capacity building, power with refers to collective consciousness and power over refers to conflict between powerful and powerless. According to UNICEF - (1994) women empowerment involves access to resources, awareness rising and control.

In India, women were treated as equals of their counterpart in the reach and enlighten societies of the past. The status of rural women in North East is comparatively better than women in thd rest of India, both in the tribal as well as the non-tribal societies of the region-Women can empower themselves through their active involvement in different fields of the society. When a woman is empowered she develops self-confidence and self esteem which leads to the overall development. Empowered women always have various opportunities in their lives and can utilize it to its full potential.

Socio-Cultural Determinants of Women Empowerment

There are number of socio-cultural and demographic factors that have influence on women empowerment. There are as follows:

(1) Education of Women: In earlier studies education was used as the indirect measures of women empowerment. It is assumed that educational attainment helps the women to be empowered by building many earning capability among them, developing confidence to force challenges, enhancing ability to make decisions regarding themselves and their intimates. All these things lead women to empowerment.

(2) Women's Age: Women perform different role in her life cycle 1e from daughter to daughter- in law and from mother to mother-in law during this transition she has to face different situations and experiences. In this regard Mason (1986) indicates that life long experience makes women able to speak for her rights. As her children grow older and get married she becomes mother in law and this status also awards her authority over her daughter in law. These view indicate that with the passes of time even a powerless women becomes empowered.

(3) **Women's Paid Job Involvement:** Women involvement in paid job/business and other income generating activities are assumed to lessen their economic dependency, provide more control over resources and enhance their participation in decision making as well as their mobility. Women involvement in paid jobs can be effective only if they have full control over their earning, otherwise it is just an addition to their responsibilities without any meaningful gain.

(4) **Family Type:** Empowerment is considered to be influenced by the type of family- It is commonly perceived that women belonging to nuclear families have relatively more choices in their life to practice rather than the women who belongs to a joint family.

(5) **Social Networking:** Women's social networking or non family group affiliation have some influence on women's empowerment Social networking provides women a window of opportunities to discuss their issues and to work out their solution. In these connection, Cochran (1986) argued that social networking and support groups were prerequisite for individuals to enhance their empowerment Social networking is also necessary for women's mental and psychological health which is essential for empowerment.

(6) **Dowry & Property Given by Parents to Their Daughters:** Rao and Bloch (1993) pointed out the importance of dowry given by the parents to their daughters at the time of marriage. They mentioned that dowry was an important element in securing a women in her in law's or husbands home. Parveen (2007) in her recent study, indicates that 84% of women were in favour of dowry and remaining 16% of women were against dowry and they wanted anti-dowry laws. Huge majority of women favouring dowry, indicated that women

give importance to dowry as they feel themselves comfortable with dowry in their in law's or husband's house.

(7) **Women's Awareness About Their Rights:** Women's awareness about their rights and practices of these rights is considered to have positive influence on women's empowerment. Therefore, in order to be empowered, women must be able to understand what their rights are and how these are being exploited This can only be achieved by increasing the level of awareness among women about their rights and practices of these rights.

(8) **Political Participation:** Political participation is assumed as one of the determinants of empowerment because political participation provides women a space for exercising their strength and opportunities for choosing the leaders who have abilities to solve their problems and commitment to reduce gender disparity. Oxaal and Baden (1997) explained that political empowerment of women is imperative for women's empowerment, because greater number of women in politics will support women cause at every level. Therefore, there was a need to initiate capacity building programmes for local councilors.

(9) **Religious Tendency:** Active participation of women in religious groups for welfare and fluid rising provides them skill and add to their abilities that could bring positive change in their status (Flora, 1975). It is obvious that following the religious practices is not enough for women's empowerment For this purpose knowledge about religion is also necessary for women in order to protect them from exploitation of men in the name of religion and to understand the difference between religious obligations and cultural rituals

(10) **Urban/Rural Area and Local Level Facilities:** Kabeer (2001) argued that context or locality explains variation in women autonomy, women agency (ability) is largely shaped by social context rather than individual characteristics. Women in the rural area have to face more difficulties and cross many cultural barriers for the attainment of education. So, it can be concluded that women in urban setting, enjoy better authority that has been inculcated by education as compared to their counterparts in rural setting.

(11) **Husband's Co-operation:** Co-operation of husbands is vital for empowering women because it is assumed that husband's co-operation set supportive atmosphere for wives to achieve good status in household. Husband and wife's emotional attachment also helps wife in acquiring good status in her husband's house. In other words emotional relation of husband wife and democratic atmosphere within family, help women to be empowered.

(12) **Media Exposure:** Mass media and inter personal communication is an important tool for women's empowerment. Radio and television can create awareness among women about their rights and bring gender equality through dramas and other interesting programmes.

(13) **Willingness for Change:** Government efforts and contribution of NGO's is necessary to empower women. However, without active participation of women, all the efforts of government on. NGO's cannot bring sufficient change in women's status. For active participation, women should have some inner feelings for change because these feelings motivate them to lake action. Women should set their own plans for building positive self image and critical thinking, in order to empower themselves.

Education and Women Empowerment

Education is considered as a gateway towards empowerment. It produces opportunities and choices for Women. Empowered women can play role in the social revolution because they know the role &, and duties towards the society which leads to development. Therefore, in recent times empowerment of women has became a serious area of study, because women from a large component of human resources of our country. They are potential contributors towards development of social, economic, cultural and political activities of an area or the country. In order that women understand their status of affairs and act upon to bring about a change, they need to be educated. Therefore, education has been recognized as important for empowerment of human beings. It is the single essential factor required before and after all social, economic, political or legal framework of women empowerment- Educated women today realize the evils of their customs which are detrimental to women. Today they despise the system of child marriage, bride-price, polygamy etc. In these contexts Indian government is making good efforts for promoting girls education. Recently they have launched “Saakshar Bharat Mission for Female Literacy.” This mission aims to bring down female illiteracy by half of its present level. Thus women’s education should be taken as a serious issue

Findings

From the above discussion it is clear that the status of women in the states of NER is better than the status of women in rest of India. But due to various constraints and burden of responsibilities women do not able to step up towards the door of growth. Especially when it comes to the backward states their development gets a hindrance. Some of them are mentioned below:–

(1) **Gender Discrimination:** Gender discrimination is one of the biggest problem which female faces

Whether it is a home or workplace, from womb to tomb the subordination is prevailing.

(2) **Early Marriage:** Early marriage is one of the chief barriers which hinder the girls further studies. The anxiety of parents towards the girls future becomes hiriderance in her development. It can be seen more in the rural areas where lack of awareness is existing.

(3) **Early Earnings:** In the backward areas supplementing the basic needs which can be fulfilled through earning of the family is more important rather than gaining education and moving towards empowerment. In such situation the education becomes burden on the family.

(4) **Social Discrimination:** The social discrimination also has its roots. Boys are always assets for the family and girls is liability, as a result of this no importance is given to the education of girls.

(5) **Traditional Values and Norms:** Traditional values and norms also play an important role. All the sacrifices are done by women only because of the patriarchal society. Women are supposed to keep all the religious beliefs of the generation. These values lead them to be more subordinate towards met-

(6) **Household Activities:** The prevailing notion among the society is that women solely can look after the household work and also take care of her children. This conception increases her burden of double work and ultimately women do not get time for her who again results into health issues.

Suggestions

Government should take appropriate steps with the participation of masses in order to bring the girl child to the main stream of education. The policies which are designed should go hand in hand. Every women related issues are important to consider by increasing their collective power.

- The parents of girl child belonging to poor families must be specially educated to understand the importance of education for their girl child as base for women empowerment.
- To construct consciousness concerning rights and responsibilities relating to laws governing to women's status in the society.
- To help women to achieved financial feasibility through literacy.
- Women to be given social security.
- Societal attention ought to be given to women in the complicated and difficult circumstances like domestic violence, social discrimination, early marriage, dowry etc.
- Persuade changes in laws relating to ownership of property and inheritance so as be gender just.
- Any policies or programmes which are framing even at the grassroots levels should be gender just.
- Building a constructive image of women in the society and recognizing their contribution in social, economic and political sphere.
- If possible, media campaigns should also be done highlight the issues of women. Others will also understand the importance of it.

Conclusion

After going through this discussion it can be understood that empowerment is a tool for development. Women always had to claim for equal status for themselves in the family and society. They must change the patriarchal attributes and the ideology of subordination of men towards them. Women should be educated to comprehend that they require a change for the betterment of themselves. To empower women in all spheres, efforts have to be taken to break the old mythology about women helplessness, lack of drive and enthusiasm in order to reach the highest of credit. The change of mindset for both male and female is necessary. Only government will not be able to achieve the target of women empowerment and development.

Now a days, many policies have been introduced by the government but still there is a gap which needs to be fulfilled. Common man should also understand the need of it. After all it is clear from the study that education is the only answer for women empowerment.

Reference

1. Sangeeta Barthakur Tamuli : (2014) Women empowerment in North-East India. EBH publishers (India).
2. Pradip Kumar Sarma & Bhaskor Jyoti Barthakur (2014) Women Empowerment in Assam. Published by Akash Singha for Nebedita Publications. Guwahati —7810063.
3. Ram Krishna Mandal & Minto LIe Women in North-East India. Mittal Publication, New Delhi.
4. Dr. Birendra Deka, Dr. Mukunda Sarmah, Bobita Das, History and Development of Indian Education. Arun Prakashan, College Hostel Road, Guwahati 781001.
5. Minaskhi Bora, Ajit Konwar, Dipjyoti Buragohain, Vigumoni Nath, "Bharatiya Itihashat Mohila" Arun Prakashan, Panbajar Guwahati.
6. International Journal of Research in Engineering IT and Social Sciences. ISSN 2250 0556, Impact Factor 6452, Volume 6 Issue 64, April 2016.

Index

C

D

E

F

G

K

L

M

Q

R

S